CREATIVE
HOSPITALITY

Creative Hospitality

MARLENE D. LEFEVER

TYNDALE HOUSE PUBLISHERS, INC., WHEATON, ILLINOIS

Dedicated to
three of our favorite guests
THELMA MYERS
CAROL RISLEY
and
MARC RISLEY

Recipes by
JACK RICHARD RISLEY

With special appreciation to
some of his favorite cooks
CAROL RISLEY
SANDRA FENTON
and
SUE BARR

These party ideas
have worked for my husband
and me. Our goal in
sharing our collection is that
each idea will be
reproduced in other Christian
homes. If an idea works,
why should it be one of a kind?
Unlike great works of art,
the more reproductions made
of a party, the greater
the value. May each new host
take these ideas and
explode them creatively—in
home after home, until
our churches can honestly
display the sign, *Our Friendly,*
Christ-filled Church.

"Christ to Earth" (see page 103)
originally appeared in "Truth
and Countertruth," © 1978
David C. Cook Publishing Co.,
Elgin, IL 60120. Used by
permission.
"The Lord Walks Guard Beside
Me" (see page 114) is
reprinted from TURNABOUT
TEACHING, by Marlene D.
LeFever, © 1973 David C. Cook
Publishing Co., Elgin, Il 60120.
Used by permission.
Library of Congress Catalog
Card Number 79-92967
ISBN 0-8423-0489-4, paper
Copyright © 1980
by Marlene D. LeFever
All rights reserved
First printing, July 1980
Printed in the United States of
America

CONTENTS

ONE   MY CHURCH MY FAMILY   9

TWO   THE BIGGER THE BETTER   17
(and not necessarily more work)

THREE   SLIGHTLY SMALLER   39
(and not a bit less fun)

FOUR   TOUCH ANOTHER GENERATION   77

FIVE   PROJECT PARTIES   99
Three parties that can spill over into your church worship service

SIX   GOD BLESS OUR HOME   123

SEVEN   SPECIAL HOLIDAY CELEBRATIONS   147

EIGHT   LET THERE BE SHOWERS   193

FOREWORD
KAREN BURTON MAINS
Author, *Open Heart, Open Home* and *Karen! Karen!*

What a wide variety of homes have welcomed me as a guest in these past years! I have eaten in public housing or in spacious Gold Coast apartments. I have spent delightful evenings in mansions and contemporary single-family houses, in communes and one-room walkups. I have dined beside swimming pools and backyard running brooks, looked out to the mountains or the deserts or the sea foaming on the sands. My hosts have been pastors and businessmen, single career women, missionaries and internationals, American government personnel or foreign oil representatives.

The styles of serving may have varied and recipes may have run the gamut from an elaborate four-course meal served by maids to a cup of water offered when there was literally nothing else to give. Yet I have become expert at detecting the common element in all these occasions. I know when I have been in the home of one who has the true gift of hospitality.

I can tell if Christian hospitality has been present simply by the way I feel when I leave. I feel cherished and healed and rested and equipped. I feel enabled, because of the time shared, to go ahead with joy and do the task at hand. I feel as though I have partaken of something of the spirit of the hospitable Christ.

None have ministered to me more than Marlene LeFever and her husband Jack Risley. I admire her creative energy and his unique way of approaching the world visually. These two combine their skills with an admirable courage which I applaud. It is a courage that plunges into lives, invites in strangers, and insists that grown people play children's games in order to deepen relationships; a courage which does not hesitate to combine thinkers and doers and sojourners in incredible social mixture.

It excites me to recommend Marlene's book because all of my family have been ministered to by some of these functions. We have come away knowing that hospitality has been present: because we are warmed and stretched, delighted or weary from laughter. How often, while reading the manuscript, I have caught myself thinking, "What a marvelous idea! That's a tool I can use to share Christ in my local body (or extended family or neighborhood)." I suspect most readers will feel the same.

This is a book that *practically* encourages hospitality. As you read it, may you soon find yourself well on the way toward comforting, and cherishing, and healing, and resting, and equipping. May you know more, through these tools and recipes and ideas, of what it means to share the spirit of the hospitable Christ.

1

MY CHURCH
MY FAMILY

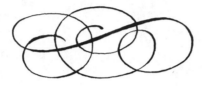

THE DOXOLOGY ENDED. There was a moment of quiet reflection while the organ played. And then the pastor made his announcement.

"I'd like to apologize for the crush of people in the foyer during the transition from the second to third services," he said. "Let's try a new traffic pattern. Those over here should file out the side door to the parking lot while those coming to the next service will use the rear doors."

His plan made sense. On recent Sundays, the meeting and greeting of crowds going two different directions had caused a terrible jam. But I felt incomplete as I followed the others in my row, duck-like out that side door. Why? *There was no space for friendship to happen.* Once out the door and into the Illinois cold, we scurried to our cars. The planned exit underlined a deeper problem in many congregations. We might rub shoulders on tight pews, but we are not rubbing lives. During the services we might fellowship with God in a special way. Yet unless we're deepening friendships and making the opportunity to meet new friends, the Christian experience isn't whole.

Christian fellowship must mean that I am growing in my understanding of my Lord, becoming more in tune with his thoughts regarding life. In addition, fellowship with God also means that I am demonstrating and receiving love from other Christians in my family —my family of God.

While I was a child, church family time was Sunday afternoon. Lunch conversation would usually center around the question, "Who should we visit this afternoon?" Quite often that question would answer itself when we heard a car pull into our driveway and we would rush out to see which friends had decided to spend their Sunday with us.

My favorite family to visit was the Gehmans. They had kids just the right age, and they had a barn where we could build tunnels in the hay. When we were tired, we could sit in the living room or on the porch and listen to our parents retell stories, share recipes, talk about the weather's effect on crops.

Looking back I realize I took one of the unique aspects of these visits for granted—people always seemed glad when we drove up. Visiting and sharing our lives was the right thing to do. How else would people spend a Sunday afternoon!

Christian fellowship was easier then, in Lancaster County. We all came from Mennonite background. For several generations, our lives had woven themselves around and through each other's. Farming and its support occupations made common topics easy to find. And of course there were always the memories of courting days.

In my quiet Sunday corner, I sat and allowed my history to catch up with me and soak in. I know how Ira, the fire chief in Bird-in-Hand, was burned. And there was the day my father showed up at my mother's door wearing knickers and she called the date off. And the stories of Jake and Nellie's misadventures with their horse and buggy.

Now I'm several decades and thousands of miles from my homogeneous community. Church seems less like a word for family and more like a building on Blanchard Road. "The Family of God" describes better a song I sing than the people I love.

Realistically, I know I'll never reproduce the types of church friendships my parents had—friendships that literally lasted from birth to death. Today people move—yearly, every three years. Has the transient church killed the possibility of church family? I find myself involved with a few close friends, but what about the other 150 people who sit in my church and sing "We Are One in the Spirit"—true theologically, but experientially?

Have you ever had my experience of walking up to someone after the service and saying, "Good morning. Provocative sermon, wasn't it?"

"Yes."

"You're new here, aren't you?" I rattle on, "I do hope you'll come back again next Sunday."

Nervous laugh. "I've been coming for three months."

My turn for a nervous laugh.

Sound familiar? But how can we get to know each other's faces and at least enough about each other to feel comfortable talking or even disappointed when we miss seeing each other in services?

My husband Jack and I have grappled with that question, and the place we decided to start was with parties—planned occasions in our home which are designed primarily to help church people feel like family.

In fact, church parties were one reason we decided to get married in the first place! We had both been quite happy single for over thirty years, so we

approached our joining in a less emotional way than we might have if we had been younger. We made lists! Seriously! We listed all the benefits of our possible marriage and all the benefits of our remaining single. After prioritizing the lists, we had a pretty good idea how important marriage was to us. High on our list was church hospitality. Together we felt we could further the idea of the church as family more successfully than we could singularly. Don't get me wrong. Church parties were certainly not our only reason for getting married. We love each other and grin a lot in our approval of God's choice for us.

Over the past four years of our marriage, we have had dozens of parties —little ones for three or four people, right up to an enormous Thanksgiving party at which we never did count all the people who came. We guess somewhere between fifty and seventy—there were a lot of children! No, we didn't rent the civic center for it. We lived, at the time, in a four-room apartment. When our neighbor across the hall saw the crush, she opened her doors and increased our room space to eight. But more about that later.

SET A GOAL

For most of the party ideas I'll share, I'll give rather complete directions. It will be possible for you to duplicate the fun we had at our special church events. However, you'll have a lot more fun, and probably better parties, if you tailor what you do to your own family's needs. Add original ideas; augment mine. If you're like I was, you'll be scared half to death the first time you invite people you have yet to know. But after that first evening, things will get progressively easier as you push your church family toward the pleasure of knowing they belong together.

One important part of our fellowship times that I would like you to duplicate is the setting of goals. The goal is the reason for the evening—what you want to see happen during those several hours. Jack and I usually talk about our goals together and quite often write them down.

Each party idea here has a suggested goal, but this goal might not perfectly fit what you want to happen. So rethink each—if it's right, guide your guests toward it; if it could be better for you, have fun rewriting.

Writing goals is not difficult. We follow this sequence:

1. Jack and I talk and pray about our fellowship idea. What needs to be done? Who might need just this sort of activity about now?
2. Then we write what we want to have happen. Careful here. What you write has to be measurable; at the end of the party, you have to be able to say, "Yes, that happened," or, "No, that goal was not reached."

A poor goal might sound great. For example, "I want the sixteen people from my Sunday school class to have fun together." But that goal is almost impossible to measure. It would be better to say, "I want everyone in my Sunday school class to spend time talking with everyone else."

You can see if that goal is met. And probably if tight groups of special friends open enough to include all sixteen people, everyone will also have fun together.

You have some control of the group's reaching a measurable goal. For example, you see the football four gathering in a corner to talk over the season's possibilities to the exclusion of other guests. If your goal is total group mixing, you could bring over an unathletic couple and introduce them into the conversation. You can note the shyness of another and spend time alone with that person helping her feel at ease before you work her into a larger group.

Sometimes I've set fantastic goals, and the parties have been flops. As I analyzed what happened, I realized that my parties and goals didn't mesh. I should have asked myself if the party I was planning could ever produce the results I wanted from it. A look at the activities and my mix of people would have told me no.

If I want people to talk with people they have never talked with before, I'd better begin with a de-icer that will force them to mix in unthreatening, successful ways. If I want singles to enjoy the evening, I have to plan my activities with this goal in mind. If there are children at the party and my goal is to help families meet families, I must make certain that the activities are fun across age levels.

All this is programmed. I have picked the direction I think the party should go. Interestingly, it sometimes surprises me and takes off in directions I never dreamed—and people are interacting and having fun. Great! I try not to chase a party with my goals, but rather follow its enthusiasm. But this type of switch rarely happens. In fact, it almost never happens in a group of all-church people who don't know each other well. Things start stiff, and we make an effort to program that stiffness out of the evening.

"Why is it so many of our non-Christian friends add life to group situations, and our Christian friends stick closely to their cliques?" my husband asked. Unfair, because he was talking about our most gregarious secular friends and two of our shiest Christian friends. But in a general way, he had a point. On the whole, non-Christians seem more at ease than Christians in social situations. They often start conversations; they include newcomers in groups; they are more skilled at small talk. Perhaps they begin learning these skills at junior high and senior high dances and continue to cultivate them in the happy hour setting.

Now, remember. I'm talking about that first encounter—the party encounter —the let's-get-acquainted evening. I know many party-imperfect Christians who on a one-to-one depth level are fantastic. I have shared my deepest doubts with them and feel their empathy and love. Of course that concern for the individual is much more important in the long run than carrying on a good conversation at a party.

Still if those fun and fellowship evenings don't get people moving toward each other, few of the deep friendships will be started. And Christians will continue to complain, "My church is so cold, unfriendly. It just isn't meeting my needs."

We invited Nancy and Ed, a couple we'd never met, to one of our parties. Their names had been on a church list of regularly attending students. When we met them at the door, we actually had to introduce ourselves to each other.

Jack got them involved in a small group, and then, in the rush of the evening, we didn't have much more contact with them.

As they were leaving, Ed told me, "In this one evening, we have met more people than we have in several months of Sundays. To be honest, we haven't been real pleased with the church and were considering finding another. But after tonight, I guess we won't be looking anymore."

We never became best friends with this couple, but oh, the wonderful things we learned from them—about their British homeland, about the best way to make English trifle, about how they could show love and respect toward each other in a social situation.

Perhaps that evening they found others who would eventually become their best friends. We became part of their larger circle of just friends. And that "just friends" circle can never be too large.

CONVERSATION STARTERS

How do we get conversations started among people who are not used to talking to one another? Many of them may have God and the same church in common—and nothing else.

We have suggested a number of techniques, many of them described in detail with the party ideas. For example, at one party we built a mound of construction paper, glue, tape, material scraps, sequins, and anything else we could find. As people arrived, we sent them to the pile to make nametags that told something about themselves. Before dinner, each person was to find out all he could about ten people's nametags.

Of course, the tags were totally unimportant. What was important was the part they played in getting people to walk up to strangers and say, "Tell me about your nametag." From that line, they were only minutes away from, "What do you think the president's move in China will mean to missions?" or "Do you have any idea how much attic insulation I really ought to have?" Great friendships from ridiculous nametags grow! The nametag makes the first approach easy—that first step many people might not be willing to take without it.

Another frustrating, effective way to mix people at the beginning of an evening is to give everyone ten toothpicks when he arrives. Explain that his objective is to get everyone else's toothpicks. He does this by taking one toothpick from anyone who says the word "I." The person with the most toothpicks at the end of a specified time (no more than twenty minutes) wins. Of course, to win each must engage others in conversation. How else will a person collect enough picks to win? It's a funny and stupid game. But the point is, it works. It gets Christians involved with others in their church.

WHO TO INVITE

We have divided those who attended our church into groups: 1. Singles (A group —college students; B group—other singles). 2. Married couples (A group— with children; B group—without children). 3. Christians and non-Christians (or very new Christians and older Christians).

Then we mix the categories.

For the past four years of our marriage, our biggest concern has been for the B group of singles. Both Jack and I had been single for a long time, and we were personally aware of how some of our single friends felt:

"We're not accepted by the married people in the church. I would give anything to spend an evening with little kids —just playing with them like an uncle would. Short of just bluntly inviting myself over, this isn't going to happen."

"I overheard one of the ladies of the church saying, 'I don't have any single friends. I don't think we'd have a thing to talk about. Actually, they scare me.' What am I? Some sort of freak?"

"I feel like a misfit. Always an uneven number."

"I'm more at home in singles bars than at most church functions. There people don't place me in a category labeled different. In fact, I feel like my stock goes up at a bar."

Jack and I wanted our home to be a place where singles could come and meet each other—comfortably, without necessarily pairing off, but with the opportunity to talk socially with other men and women.

That social contact is extremely important to the single adult. I know. When I first came to work in Illinois after spending three years as a missionary teacher in Japan, I didn't know anyone my age. I suffered from peer starvation! Sure, I would have enjoyed dating, but my need was more basic than that. I didn't have a single friend my age—male or female—to whom I could talk.

I'll never forget the first Sunday I visited Circle Church in Chicago. Two single women greeted me and asked if I would like to go out to lunch with them. Would I! I felt like the famine was over. I would have willingly paid for their complete dinners, including dessert, just to express my appreciation.

"Always singles at our parties." That rule has been rather strictly enforced by Jack and me in our apartment, and now, in our first home.

We often mix married couples and singles—a less-than-earthshakingly creative idea. And yet, for some people, it represents the first time they have ever crossed the lines between the groups.

Sometimes we will mix some of our church friends with others outside the church. This can be ticklish. In no way do we want neighbors and others to feel we have invited them in order to propagandize our faith. Yes, Christ is a part of our home and our marriage and the lives of many of our friends. That's no secret. We want our other friends to someday share our enthusiasm willingly, not because they were invited to a social occasion and unsuspectingly buttonholed and forced into a decision they do not wholeheartedly accept.

One evening we had a game party going on in three of the four rooms of our apartment. By drawing names, couples had chosen other couples as opponents in board games. Suddenly in

the middle of the second game, one of the women screamed an expletive that hadn't been heard in that home since we moved in. Her partner had made a wrong move, and she had uttered her normal response.

Later a friend who is uncomfortable with the church told Jack, "I was impressed by what happened. Here was this swearing dame sitting across from a preacher and his wife. No one fainted or delivered a sermon."

It was this woman's first time in our home. Perhaps there will be another time more right for sharing how we feel about the name she used so lightly, but that time was definitely not right in the middle of a party.

Most of our parties are aimed directly at the people who attend our church. Some of the names come from the membership and church directory list. Others are first timers who sign a visitor's card. Still others are students who attend only when school is in session.

"I was amazed when I got your invitation," Julie told us. "It read that you had invited a group from your church. I'd only visited twice—the two times I've been in church during the year my divorce became final. I was hurting and God seemed far away.

"At the party, people talked and laughed. They included me. That evening I met people who are now my best friends. More important, God and I smiled at each other again."

Julie verbalized her feelings at a time when Jack and I were wondering if it was worth all the effort. She is living proof that God was using our gift for hospitality.

2

THE BIGGER
THE BETTER
(and not necessarily more work)

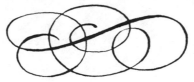

HOLD IT! If you're going to whip right past these ideas because you've got a limited budget and a small home, don't.

Never underestimate the number of people who can have a great time in a small place. Most of the ideas in this section were tested in our four-room apartment. Of course, we had wall-to-wall people, but no one seemed to mind. In fact, people mixed more easily at these parties than they did at our smaller ones.

I think the noise level has something to do with it. When a room is filled with a number of different groups, all talking at once, my individual pauses aren't noticed as much. I can relax and have a better time. Noise makes me less self-conscious. Years ago I worked as a reporter. My desk was in the middle of unwalled space in the city room. Twenty typewriters all going at once, and I could work. Every once in a great while, everyone would hit a stopping point at the same time and the room would be silent. People would look up nervously and we would all lose several minutes before we could build up the level of comfortable noise again. Big parties usually have comfortable noise built right in.

I also like the casual fun of a large party. There are never enough chairs, so people just drape themselves all over the place. When I first started giving parties, I would count the number of chairs I had and invite just enough bodies to fill them. That didn't work. Have you ever looked at a room full of people all sitting on chairs? They tend to place the chairs in lines around the wall —eight couples hugging the wall. It's awful. In that setup everyone becomes part of the whole conversation—after all, we're all in this square circle. That means with my eight couples, I get to talk 1/16th of the time. That's a lot of quiet. Dreary party. So now I take half the chairs I own, stack them somewhere, and force people to break into comfortable conversation groups. I like it; I get to talk more.

Big parties can cost money, but there are ways to get around that. Covered dishes, dessert only, poor box at the door (and yes, we've done this). Careful not to let food become the main purpose for the evening. Jack's a gourmet cook, and every once in a while, he insists on sharing the fruits of this hobby, but food should be kept in proper perspective. Use it. Food can help you reach a goal. It's easier to talk with someone you hardly know when you're cracking and eating peanuts together.

For almost all big parties, we share the food responsibility. I write on the invitation—bring Jello, or we're planning a smörgasbord of desserts. I can hardly wait to see what you bring.

Sharing the work means I survive to enjoy my own party. But it also means that my guests will be more committed to having a good time because they have a small investment of their time and money in the evening.

I remember one bachelor who said he was baking his mother's best chocolate cake as his contribution to a party. He had called Maryland to get the recipe, and Jack was going to be green with envy. The party was half over when he finally arrived carrying a squatty boxed cake straight from the baker. "I almost didn't come," he said. "My cake turned

out soupy, and I was mortified. But
then I remembered this great Swedish
bakery across town. So I rushed over and
bought this." Sure, I was sorry that
he didn't feel free enough to show up
without his soupy offering. But I was also
pleased that he was so involved with
his party contribution—even to the point
of figuring that the party just couldn't
get by without a cake from him. And,
by the way, the town he drove across to
get the cake was Chicago!

THE EASY WAYS
Do things the easiest way possible.

Cleaning—Do the heavy stuff in the
early part of the week so that on the day of
the big event all you need to do is
pick up. With some parties, I was so
exhausted by the time the guests arrived
that I enjoyed nothing about the
evening except the closing of the door
behind the last guest on his way home.
That was silly. If I had paced myself, what
a difference it would have made!

Lists—Once again, they make things
easier because you aren't plagued
with last-minute flashes of things that
absolutely have to be done. I make
lists for everything—perhaps overdoing
it a bit. I start with lists of ideas for
the party, lists of people who might
enjoy coming, lists of people who
RSVP'd, lists of food everyone will be
bringing, lists of the week and the day-
before chores.

Husbands—Or wives, as the case may
be. If you're married, giving a party
is something you both do. Jack and I plan
together, work together on the ideas,
and in the end enjoy the party together.

It makes the whole process easier when
one person doesn't have to do everything.
I clean better than he does. Somehow
he has never considered the fact that
baseboards get dusty and it makes sense
to clean them, with all those guests
coming to sit on the floor. On the other
hand, I don't enjoy cooking. He takes
that responsibility out of my hands. It's
really OUR party. Hospitality is not a
feminine word.

Singles—Consider sharing the work
for your hospitality evenings too. Pair up
with a girl friend or boyfriend. Divide
the work and share the evening's fun.
Two other friends and I made a Japanese
dinner for about forty people from
our church. A mammoth job, but divide
the work three ways and the feat is
no longer amazing.

ALL UNDER ONE ROOF
An Unusual Progressive Dinner
What follows is an outline of how we did
our All-Under-One-Roof progressive
dinner. Follow our pattern exactly, if you
wish. Or use it as a starting point
for ideas and jump off from here into
your unique party.

Goal: That singles and marrieds in our
church converse with each other in
comfortable, conversational settings.

Basic idea: Plan a progressive dinner in
your own home. People will progress
from one room to another for each
course. With each table or room change,
they will eat with a different group
of people.

INVITATION IDEA

PROGRESS WITH US FOR DINNER
from the Living Room to the Bedroom to the Dining Room

When:

Where:

*Why: To meet other married and single people
in our church.*

*ALL UNDER ONE ROOF, we'll supply the
food, but friendship is totally up to you.*

All-Under-One-Roof Progressive Dinner cuts down on the amount of time people spend driving from one house to the next. The party is ecologically sound! It also forces people to break predictable friendship groupings and meet new people since table groups are assigned.

We pulled off this progressive dinner in three of the four rooms in our apartment. We set up two small tables in the living room, a larger one in the bedroom, and of course we used the dining room table. Jack and I each took a room that would be ours to serve, and we asked our friend Caroline to work the third. We three couldn't participate in the meal since our jobs involved serving it and running back and forth to the kitchen for refills.

But our primary responsibility was to encourage people to interact.

Before the party, the three of us went over a number of gimmick topics we could use if it was obvious that a table group wasn't working. We would throw out questions like these:

"What's your opinion of house churches?"

"Why don't you find out something from the person on your left that he has never told anyone at our church before?"

"What kind of animal have you always thought you were most like? Why?"

My invitation mix was half singles and half married. Of the singles I tried to get half women and half men. At each table I wanted some married people and a mix of male and female singles. My party limit was determined by how many tables I could set and how much food Jack could make in our small kitchen.

When a person arrived, he was given a program indicating where he would sit for each course. He might change tables or rooms or stay in the same room and have his table people change. It was great fun trying to put the whole pattern together. A program card would look like this:

ROBERT RICHARDSON
Soup and Salad—Bedroom Table
Main Course—Dining Room Table
Dessert—Small Table in the
Living Room

We planned three courses—three moves for each person. The courses were soup and salad, main course, and dessert. We allowed about a half hour for each course, and about five minutes between courses for people to find where they were to go next.

I did not arrange who would sit where at each table. How the group placed itself was its decision. It was interesting that for the first course, most married people grouped themselves at one end of the table and the singles at the other. By the main course people were a little more mixed, and by dessert, my goal had been reached.

At our party, the first course was supposed to include homemade cauliflower soup. Jack was taking a soup course at a cooking school and this was to be his one creative touch for the meal. To this day, we have no idea why the soup turned rancid, but just minutes before the guests arrived we discovered it tasted slightly carbonated. We discussed how many might die if we served it, and decided not to take the chance. Out it went, and as the front doorbell rang, Jack was dashing out the back door to the supermarket for cans of soup.

We had chopped onions for garnish on the cauliflower, and it went into the canned soup. Would you believe we got all sorts of compliments on our soup— and we accepted every one!

Depending on your group, you may want to implement these ideas.

1. Why not pray after each course? The people at each table would elect someone to thank God for the food that had been eaten and especially for the fellowship at the table during that half hour.
2. You might want to put questions for discussion under different plates.
   Here are some ideas for questions:
   "Share something you like about our church. Then pick someone else at your table to do the same."
   "What's your least favorite way to spend a vacation?"
   "If you had a million dollars, what would be some of the things you would do with it after you paid your tithe?"
   "Go around your table telling everyone's name. If you can't remember the name, tell something that you've picked up about the person during this course."

Questions like these are easy to write yourself. If the question can be answered in a single word, it's probably not a good one—it's over too quickly and doesn't force the person answering to share much about himself. Try to think of questions that demand paragraph answers, and pick subjects that might spark conversation.

You may not need conversation starters at some of your tables, but my motto for parties is "Be Prepared." When a group of people are eating in dead silence, I get the urge to serve that cauliflower soup.

Be Prepared.

PROGRESSIVE DINNER
RECIPE IDEAS
Meal designed to serve 24
First Course—Soup and Salad

CAROL'S CORN CHOWDER

12 large onions, chopped
8 medium potatoes, diced
4 cups chopped celery with leaves
1 1/2 teaspoon salt
12 cups milk
4 cans cream style corn
Cover onions, potatoes, celery with water. Add salt. Cook until tender. Add milk and corn, and reheat. Add salt and pepper to taste.

HERBED SALAD

4 heads lettuce, torn
1 package fried bacon (crispy), crumbled
1 dozen hard-boiled eggs, crumbled
Place bacon and egg crumbles over the torn lettuce.

Dressing:
2 cups salad oil
4 small onions, sliced
2 cups white vinegar
3 Tablespoons mustard
1 cup sugar
3 Tablespoons lemon juice
Salad herbs
Mix and herb to taste. For example, add 2 Tablespoons of oregano or 2 teaspoons of dill weed. Refrigerate four days to allow flavor to penetrate the mixture.

Main Course

APRICOT CHICKEN

6 chickens cut in pieces
3 large jars apricot preserves
3 large jars French dressing
4 packages dried onion soup mix
8 Tablespoons Worcestershire sauce
Bake chicken in a buttered, uncovered baking dish for 1 hour at 350°. Mix the rest of the ingredients together, and at the end of the hour, add the sauce to the chicken. Cover tightly and cook 20 minutes longer, or until fork tender.

RICE

4 cups uncooked rice
4 5-ounce cans of water chestnuts, drained and sliced
8 cups hot water
4 Tablespoons butter or margarine.
Toast rice in a shallow casserole at 350°. Stir occasionally so rice browns evenly. Blend remaining ingredients; stir into rice. Bake covered until rice is tender and liquid is absorbed (about 30 minutes).

Add a vegetable and rolls and butter to this course, if you wish.

Dessert Course

THE RASPBERRY ANGEL

4 angel food cakes
2 pudding mixes—vanilla is best
1 large jar of raspberry jelly
Carefully slice each cake horizontally to make three layers. Fill the first layer with pudding and the second with raspberry jelly. Frost with butter frosting.

ROOTS
Covered Dish Dinner

Goal: Church family will share backgrounds, building the basis for closer friendships.

Basic idea: Invite church family adults to bring a covered dish that says something about their historical or geographical roots. Plan the whole evening around the sharing of backgrounds. As people share recipes, childhood stories, facts about grandparents, they add enormous amounts to the little most of them know about each other. The more people share, the more a feeling of family develops.

We have found that for parties that are this unusual, we need to give people some ideas of what we want them to do. This encourages them to think creatively. On this invitation, I've included Jack's and my ideas. You would want to delete ours and include your own.

The number of guests you have is limited only by floor space. You may want to supply coffee, tea, and punch, and your own Roots contribution, but the dinner will come walking through your door with your guests. (Most of our people brought a dish for from six to ten people; we had more than enough food.)

When the guests arrive, have them write their names on slips and place them in a hat for a drawing after dinner.

Give them ROOT SHEETS. Before dinner and up to the time of the drawing, they are to talk to ten different people. From each they should get the answer to one question on the ROOT SHEET.

Obviously the goal of this activity is to get people to talk. What they find out about the person's answer to a sheet question is not as important as what they say after the question has been answered.

Here are the items we had on our ROOT SHEETS. Adjust yours. You'll probably find it necessary to push people at the beginning. Let them know that there will be a time of accountability for what they have learned!

ROOT SHEET
1. Find out an interesting story about someone's grandparents.
2. Talk with a couple who each came from different parts of the country. What background quirks did they bring to their marriage?
3. Find someone who has a famous or infamous ancestor.
4. Talk with a single about a childhood experience he or she would like to pass on to future generations.
5. Share the funniest experience you can remember about a relative.
6. Find someone who has a relative who could have been rich or famous if he had followed through on an opportunity.
   (For example, I have an uncle who had an opportunity to buy the property on which Disney World now stands for only a few dollars an acre. He didn't buy because he was sure an investment in a swamp would never pay off!)
7. Find the person here who has the most living relatives he can identify by first names.
8. Find someone who has lived in at least three completely different places in

INVITATION IDEA

ROOTS COVERED DISH PARTY

*Share your roots. Dig into your personal
history and come up with a dish that tells
something about your ancestral or
geographical background.*

When:

Where:

For example:

*Marlene is French, and she'll bring a French
pastry.*

*Jack's family was from Washington; he'll
bring stewed apples.*

*Label your dish—its name and origin, and
your name. Think success!*

Bring along copies of your recipe to share.

his lifetime. Which did he like best and why?

9. Find someone who comes from the longest line of people who are in a similar trade.
10. Find a couple who, without checking with each other, can give the maiden names of the other's mother and grandmother.
11. Find someone who has an amazing childhood story and listen to it—the whole way through.
12. Ask someone to dig back into her junior high past and come up with something important that happened.
13. Get someone to share something from his personal past that made him blush.
14. Ask someone who grew up in a Christian home to share the history of his parents' or grandparents' conversion.
15. Ask someone to share a game he has played that originated in his geographic root area.

ROOTED IN CHRIST

At least a half hour before you want people to begin eating the ROOTS meal, ask three people to prepare "Rooted in Christ" prayers. The half hour will give them time to think about what they will say, and perhaps even to write the prayer. Ask one to center his prayers on thanksgiving for the church's roots. Another should praise God for her salvation roots. The third should thank God for any friendship roots that deepen or begin to grow this evening.

Sample prayers are included here. If the people you have asked to pray don't understand what you're asking them to

do allow them to read these samples. Encourage them to put their prayers into their own words.

Thanksgiving for the Church's Roots
"Lord, how excellent is your name! I praise you that your name is the foundation of our church, that we are rooted in your love. Without you, we would be nothing but hollow people meeting inside empty walls. I pray that you will guide our church's growth."

Praise for Personal Salvation Roots
"Lord, thank you that from the time I was born, I was rooted and grounded in you, as my parents shared both their love for me and for you. As I look back, there never was a time when I didn't know that you loved me. Sure, I failed you often, but those early roots were not easily torn out. Thank you, Lord, for a Christian heritage."

Praise for Friendship Roots
"Thank you, Lord, for parties. For the times when we as a body of Christ can get together and hello and smile and get excited about each other. Keep your hand on our conversations tonight. Guide the growth of our friendship with those you have chosen to be our brothers and sisters."

Give people plenty of time to eat. Don't rush. A ROOTS supper is unique. Just the amazing array of foods should provide interesting conversation. Encourage food refills and exchange of recipes.

After the meal, use the names you collected from all the guests and placed in the hat. Draw three or four names, and ask those people to share one of the most interesting things they discovered about someone in the ROOT SHEET conversations. This type of accountability is fun and no one will be embarrassed since he is allowed to pick anything from the list to share. If he never got to number 7, no one else need know about it. He'll just share the answer he got to number 3.

At my ROOTS party, I gave prizes to the people whose names were drawn. I had small plants that had been rooted in water, so all their roots were exposed. They were silly extras that made the evening more fun.

After the planned ROOT activities were over, our guests stuck around for hours. They had no trouble at all growing friendships once the ROOTS had been planted.

ROOT RECIPES

Once in a while, you'll find that someone will draw a blank on his roots. So be prepared with a few recipes that cover large geographic areas. Supply these only when necessary—you wouldn't want someone not to come simply because he doesn't know what to bring. These recipes are simple, since usually the people who have trouble thinking of what to bring are not used to cooking.

STEWED APPLES

(Good for anyone who comes from the northern sections of the United States.)
6 apples cored and quartered
1/3 cup sugar
lump butter
cinnamon (to taste)
Add all ingredients except cinnamon to a small mount of water. Boil at low heat until apples are soft. Add cinnamon.

BANANA WALDORF SALAD

(Good for anyone who comes from the southern sections of the United States.)
3 large apples
1/2 cup celery
1/2 cup salad dressing
2 bananas
1/2 cup crumbled walnuts
lettuce
Mix ingredients and serve on lettuce. Serves 6.

FISH STEW

(Good for anyone who comes from a seacoast region.)
1 Tablespoon cooking oil
1 clove garlic, chopped
1/2 cup chopped onion
1/3 cup chopped green pepper
Sauté in a Dutch oven or a large saucepan.
1/4 pound mushrooms, sliced (optional)
2 cups cooked tomatoes
3/4 cup tomato paste
1 cup chicken broth
1 Tablespoon lemon juice
1 small bay leaf
1/2 teaspoon dried oregano
1 teaspoon sugar
3/4 teaspoon salt
1/8 teaspoon pepper
Add these ingredients to those you have sautéed. Cook uncovered for 20 minutes. Add 1-1½ pounds of flounder or other white fish, cut in large pieces. Cook 10 to

15 minutes longer, or until fish flakes easily.

Serve over rice or spaghetti. Serves 6.

TRIFLE

(Good for anyone with English background.)

1 package yellow or white cake mix
1 can fruit cocktail (any combination of fruit can be used here—bananas, strawberries, blueberries, etc.)
1 cup vanilla pudding

Bake cake. When cool, cut into large bite-sized pieces. Add the fruit, including juice, and the custard to the cake. Stir gently. Chill several hours. Can be served with a garnish of sweetened whipped cream.

CORN BREAD

(Good for a person with farming background or ancestors.)

3/4 cup cornmeal
1 1/2 cup flour
3 teaspoons baking powder
1 teaspoon salt
1/4 cup sugar
2 large eggs
1 cup milk
1/4 cup melted butter

Grease a 9″ x 9″ pan. Flour. Sift dry ingredients together. Beat eggs one half minute. Add milk and beat another half minute. Add liquid to dry ingredients. Blend. Add melted butter, and mix only until blended. Spread in pan. Bake at 375° for about 15 minutes or until golden brown. Cool about 10 minutes before loosening and cutting into squares.

YAWN!
A Board Party

Objective: Single and married people in our church will have opportunities to build friendships as they compete in simple board games.

Basic idea: Bring back a few of the old parlor games, and structure round robin games around them. After games, serve do-it-yourselves soup and salad.

PREPARATION:
Collect game boards. I never have enough, so I ask other guests to bring some along. If your friends are like mine, you might want to line up more boards than you'll need. People often forget.

I set up the games everywhere—on window seats, tables, floor. And actually, I've never been a purist about the board angle of the party. Pick Up Sticks is a great game. So are Jacks. Tiddlywinks can help adults rid themselves of a decade of inhibitions.

I number each game location.

When people come, they draw one number out of each of three bags—a red bag, a green bag, and a grocery bag. For the first game, everyone goes to the board with the number on his red tag; for the second game he goes to the one numbered on his green tag; and finally he plays the grocery bag tag.

Be careful setting this up. You have to be certain you know the number of people coming so you'll have the right number of numbers and games. You also have to be careful to have the right number of tags in each bag to successfully

INVITATION IDEA

YAWN—WE'RE "BOARD"
Come and be "board" with us.
We're planning an evening of good, old-
fashioned board games.
Come and meet our church at play.
When:
Where:
Food? Sure! We're making Whatever soup.
We'll have the stock simmering and you
bring something to add to the stock. The
soup will be what you make it.
Or, bring something to add to the lettuce.
We promise you won't be bored!

Yawn!

play different games. For example, Chinese Checkers only takes two people. So if that game is number six, you should have no more than two number six cards in each bag. You'll want four people for Sorry. So you'll need four slips with Sorry's game number in each bag.

This party mixes married and single people beautifully, and since numbers are drawn, people rarely will play the same people twice.

I allow about twenty minutes for each game. There are just three scheduled games in an evening, and that allows about an hour for the soup to simmer. After the soup and salad meal, the planned part of the evening is over. The games are only ice breakers.

At my board parties, I've found that singles were usually more at ease than couples. Great! They pulled the married people into the action, taking friendship leadership from the group that most often exercises leadership in the church.

FOOD SUGGESTIONS

This party is limited only by the size of your soup kettle! Provide the soup stock to which your guests will add the extras. Dry bouillon (dehydrated cubes) or chicken broth make excellent stock.

You may have guests ask for ideas of what to add. For the soup, you might suggest carrots, potatoes, noodles, rice, chicken pieces, turnips, corn, celery —and the list goes on.

For the salad, you could suggest beets, bean sprouts, cheese, croutons, garbanzo beans, sunflower seeds, crumbled hard-boiled eggs, green pepper, bacon bits,

turkey or ham slices, shredded carrots, olives, cauliflower—and the list goes on.

IDEAS

Before soup is served, ask a married guest to thank God for the delight and diversity in the foods he made. Ask a single guest to thank God for the delight and diversity in the people he made.

Sample Prayers:

Married Person: "We have all brought something to add to the soup and salad, Lord, and with each addition we are reminded of how much we have. What a creative God you are! Thank you for the texture of the turnip and the fine hardiness of the potato. Thank you for the common sense of lettuce and the taste of excitement the tomato adds. What fun you must have had making all these foods. We appreciate you, God, and praise you for your creativity."

Single Person: "Thank you, God, for the many different people you have brought together in our church—for people who can talk easily, for people who giggle, for those who can bear prayer burdens, for those who preach and teach. Not one of us is a carbon copy of another. And like our additions to the soup and salad, each of us adds texture and unique taste to your creation of the church. Thank you that I am part of this mix."

Name the Soup:

Why not sponsor a little contest? Everything needs a name. The group will have created a unique and totally original soup and salad. What in the world should they name their creations? Give

31

everyone three-by-five cards and ask those who wish to participate in naming the creations to put their suggestions in a box. Choose some perfectly partial judges to pick the winning names! Perhaps these winners could take home some of the leftovers.

A WORD ABOUT CUPID

I'm all for the little fellow! But with common sense. Since so many of our parties include single Christians, I want to share my perspective.

I have often invited singles I thought would enjoy each other to my parties, but what happens after they get there is up to them. Dating is healthy. If two people can meet and talk and enjoy each other at our house, and later also enjoy dating, that's grand. What better place for people to meet than in a Christian home?

Jack and I were happy single. But part of our contentment can be traced back to our friendships with other singles. Friends—girl friends and boyfriends —are a part of healthy single life.

Karen introduced Jack and me. She told him that I was the type of girl he might enjoy dating. I doubt that he would have noticed me if she hadn't pointed. But she cared enough to point. And he trusted her judgment enough to ask me to a play. We talked through the entire evening, and we haven't stopped talking since. She pointed us in the direction of friendship.

I'd even go so far as to suggest Christian obligation in this context. Whole businesses are built around providing secular places for singles to meet. My single Christian friends don't belong in a singles bar. But if the alternative is sitting at home alone, can I blame them for heading in that direction?

I have a set of rules that I usually follow in my self-appointed task of dating yenta.

First, let things happen. It's usually enough just to invite singles to the party. I provide activities that allow them to come with or without dates and not feel left out or different.

Second, don't hesitate to bring up the subject of dating. So two people never did meet at a party but they would enjoy dating—or at least I think they might. Why not suggest it? If either says no, what has he lost? What have I lost? But they rarely do.

Recently I was talking with Dale.

"I think you might enjoy meeting Skip. How would you feel about going out to dinner with him? Maybe double date with Jack and me."

"I'd be scared to death," she said.

"Does that mean no?"

"It means yes. I'd be scared, but I'd do it. It's just one evening out of my lifetime, and I think once I quit shaking, I'll have a good time."

As far as I know, not one single has ever met his mate at our parties. That's fine with me. But I do know many, many who have built friendships with other singles, and enjoyed being single more because of it.

"I haven't dated since my divorce," Jean said. "I'm lonesome, and frankly, I feel ugly. Last night I ended up playing Pick Up Sticks with Phil, and for the first time in ages I was laughing and feeling less like a loser.

32

"I lost the crazy game," she admitted. "But it was important to know that someone of the opposite sex was having a good time with me."

Third, move out of the picture. Once I've done my introduction, suggestion, or first double date, it's over. I pull out. It's important for people not to feel pressured into friendship or somehow guilty if it's obvious that my dating match was a mismatch. What happens in their relationship has nothing to do with the friendship I've built with them as individuals. Meddling can be manipulative and dangerous.

Single is wonderful. It's a life style some people elect, and others, for one reason or another, are part of. And it can be a lot more fun when it includes friendships with other singles, married couples, and families.

MYSTERY BAG SUPPER

Goal: To encourage each person from our church to talk with a large number of others, getting to know them in a casual, nonthreatening setting.

Basic idea: Everyone will pack a bag supper and include in his bag a clue to his identity. The host couple will mix up the bags before everyone picks one at random. The meal activity involves each person discovering whose bag supper he is eating.

This party is limited only by the number of people the hosts can pack in. And it's inexpensive. The hosts are responsible only for punch and coffee, and everything else is part of the bag.

This idea also makes a great replace-

ment for the traditional church covered-dish supper. I like church suppers, but often the food is cold by the time my part of the line gets served, and more important, we sit at long tables—usually with our friends who are saving us seats. So I'm limited in the people I can get to know better.

"We've just started to go to First Church," Andy told me. "Sandy's a new Christian, and the monthly church supper was her first experience with a Christian social. She was so excited, but when we got to the church, everyone seemed at home with friends. It was as though the circles were closed. We ended up sitting with the one lady in the whole church we already knew. She's great, but we had looked forward to the evening as an opportunity to increase the number of people we could greet by name."

"I wish we could have moved around a little," Sandy said. "It was almost like sitting in the pews and eating—nice long rows of Christians munching!"

Obviously an important clue to the success of the Mystery Bag Supper is being in a place where you can move about a little to check with people throughout the room about their clues. When we tried this party, I had most of the people sitting on our floors in constantly changing groupings. There were little footpaths people followed as they searched for the person behind their bag's clues.

Clues are important. Encourage people to write reasonable ones—clues that could possibly be discovered by people at the church.

For example, I'm a high school Sunday

INVITATION IDEA

MYSTERY BAG SUPPER

Shhhhhh, and follow these directions:
1. *Pack a great bag lunch*
2. *Include a clue to your identity in the bag*
3. *When:*
4. *Where:*
Mystery Question: By the end of this evening,
what new friends will you have made?

Mystery Bag Supper

school teacher, so my clue for our church might be:

Before the doxology has been sung
I get a taste of feeling young!

Now that clue doesn't give me away, but it does put me in the Sunday school somewhere, and even someone who has no idea who I am would have a starting place. He could ask others, "Are you in the Sunday school? Do you teach? Did you pack this supper?"

EXPANDING THE PARTY

Mystery Bag Supper can be the total activity of the evening, especially if it precedes the Sunday evening service. Or it can be expanded. Here are some ways to expand the mystery supper into a total mystery evening. Pick the ideas that would work best in your group. Add your own special touches of creativity.

Mystery Speaker

Announce that there are going to be three mystery speakers. In fact, the mystery is so deep that the speakers don't even know who they will be.

The mystery speaker idea has a getting-to-know-you flavor, adding a rather unique Christian emphasis. For your three speakers, pick guests who have little trouble talking in front of the group. Interview each person, using questions that will force paragraph answers. Some ideas follow.

Ask the first mystery guest speaker these questions:
(Pick someone you are certain is a Christian.)
1. Share your name. Tell how you

came to have your first name(s).
2. If you could have one contemporary person as a mystery guest in your home, who would you choose and why?
3. What might you serve this person for dinner? Why?
4. If you had about an hour with this person after dinner, what questions would you ask?
5. If Jesus were coming to your house for supper, what three very recent happenings in your life would you like to thank him for?

Ask the second mystery guest speaker these questions:
(Pick a person you know has a strong Christian witness.)
1. Share your name and give a little background on your last name.
2. If you were on a mystery plane ride and you knew you could have the plane land anywhere in the world, where would you want to land and why?
3. What are some of the things you would like to do after you land?
4. Suppose you discovered that most of the people in this country knew nothing about your God, but they all spoke your language. What things would you share with them?
5. Suppose Jesus gave you an envelope in which he had placed the mystery location where he wants you to serve him. He tells you not to open it until you are certain you are willing to be a living testimony for him. You pray, and make the decision to open the envelope. Inside is your home address along

35

with the addresses of most of the people in your immediate area (block, apartment building, small town). What things would you immediately get busy doing?

6. You get such a good response that you decide to ask God for additional helpers in your area. What qualities would you want these new workers to have? Why is each quality you mention so important?

Ask the third mystery guest speaker these questions:
(Pick someone who is active in the church.)

1. It's always been a mystery to non-Christians why we give up Sunday morning sleep to go to church. Pretend I'm a non-Christian neighbor who has just asked, "Is church really worth all the trouble you go through to get there?" Answer assuming that I'm really interested in a serious answer and it could make a difference in my life.
2. Suppose you are the mystery speaker at our Sunday evening service. No one knows you'll be speaking, but you want to do your best to get everyone out to the meeting. What things would you do to attract people's interest in the service?
3. Why do you like our church?
4. Suppose someone in your neighborhood says, "People who go to church are dull. Name me one who isn't." Go the third mile and name him three people in our church who aren't dull, and share what makes these people exciting.

5. Share two things about our church you think we should praise God for.

Some help for the interviewer:
Of course, you will pick mystery speakers who talk easily in front of people, but you still carry a lot of responsibility for keeping things light and moving. Most of the guests' questions will be easy to answer. But suppose someone has been asked to share three things and he draws a blank after two. That's fine. You can add a third, or simply move onto the next question.

Often an extemporaneous speaker will not fully develop an idea. You can help by asking, "Can you tell us more about that?" Or, "How might you go about that?"

Encourage your guest speakers. They are answering in difficult, unprepared situations. Affirm them. Saying things like this will help: "That's a very creative answer!" "What a good idea; I wish some of us would try it." "For an off-the-cuff speaker, you're excellent."

Look at the guest when he's talking. Know the questions that you will ask well enough to get involved in the speaker's contribution. Smile when it's appropriate. Encourage when necessary. Add something, if you think it would be helpful, but be careful not to steal the show from the guest. After all, you've had time to think about the questions, and he has not.

You can involve the audience. After the mystery speaker has given some good ideas, you could turn to the whole group and say, "OK, here's your chance. What would you add?"

If you get an overtalkative speaker, you may want to interrupt with the next question. Each speaker should be on stage for no more than eight minutes. This allows time for a twenty-four-minute speaking time—about your adults' listening limit.

Mystery Games
Why not use basic game plans with which people are familiar, but add a mystery twist?

MYSTERY RHYMES
Write one line of double couplet rhymes on slips of paper. Hide these slips throughout the house. Each guest should hunt until he finds one slip of paper. He then begins searching for others who found lines that rhyme with his. There are four slips in each rhyme, so there will be four people in each group. (You may also want to number each slip so people will find it even easier to decide who is in their group.)

When all four people in a group have found each other, they should arrange their rhyme in an order that makes sense and prepare to recite it to the group.

The first group to find all four of its people wins. If you have an uneven number, announce that a group may discover that all people have rhyme slips and it's still missing one or two. The whole group searches for the missing slips and will then read more than one line per person when it shares with the whole party.

Use as many of these rhymes as you need. Or if you need more, make up your own.

1. *We want you all to know*
1. *When high winds gust and blow*
1. *When falls the rain and snow*
1. *To church we still will go*

2. *It's not the living end*
2. *The rules we want to bend*
2. *It's not a sin to lend*
2. *Nursery duty to a friend*

3. *I go to hear what's written*
3. *It seems quite right and fittin'*
3. *I squirm like a baby kitten*
3. *I think I'm tired of sittin'*

4. *What is that awful wail?*
4. *The church all turns pale*
4. *The choir has missed the trail*
4. *That note's not on the scale*

5. *We've got a goodly hunch*
5. *Hashed preacher's had for lunch*
5. *Things would improve a bunch*
5. *If we'd pray before we crunch*

6. *No trouble when it's light*
6. *Sunday brings the church in sight*
6. *But something's not quite right*
6. *We can't find it Wednesday night*

7. *Gossip is the word I fear*
7. *It can burn and it can sear*
7. *But would it cost so dear*
7. *If we remembered God can hear*

MYSTERY CHARADES
Follow all the rules for charades, but set the idea around the word *mystery*—rather than the more normal categories of song titles, plays, or books.

If the two sides have difficulties thinking of mystery topics which the other side must act out, get them started with these few suggestions:

Ah, Sweet Mystery of Life
Sherlock Holmes
Agatha Christie
Murder on the Orient Express
The Hardy Boys
Nancy Drew
The Mouse Trap
The mystery guest (word)

I'VE GOT A MYSTERY
Ask a number of people to come
prepared with a mystery to share. If they
need samples, share these:
   "I lost the diamond from my ring, and
to this day I haven't found it."
   "My son has an interest in mechanics,
and there hasn't been a mechanical
person in my family for generations. It's
a mystery to me where he gets his talent."
   "I'm teaching a class of ten senior
high boys and two girls. It's a mystery to
me why the girls don't just flock in."
Before the game write the mysteries on
large cards so they can be shown to the
audience, but not those guessing what
the mystery is.
   Model "I've Got a Mystery" after the
old television program "I've Got a
Secret." Choose four panel members at
random from the guests. They each take
turns asking the person with a mystery

question about the mystery. Each
question must be answered with a yes or
no. A panelist continues asking questions
until he gets his first no. Then it's
the next panelist's turn.
   Panelists should start asking broad
questions and work down to specifics. For
example, "Does your secret involve a
person?" "A person in your family?"
"Your son, Joshua?"
   At any time during the questioning, the
host may yell *clue!* At this point, the
person with the mystery must share a
substantial clue.
   When a panelist guesses a mystery,
award that panel member a small prize,
retire him, and choose another member.

Mystery Collection
Ask guests to put their Christ-centered
project ideas into a bag. Explain that
one of these projects will be chosen and
the offering will go to that project.
These projects might include special
church-related things or special gifts to
missionaries, etc.
   After the offering has been taken and
counted, have someone draw a project,
sight unseen, from the bag and read it.
Appoint someone to make sure the
donation is delivered.

3

SLIGHTLY
SMALLER
(and not a bit less fun)

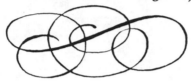

RUTH WAS THE MOST amazing hostess I've known. She lived in a tiny one-room apartment, just barely big enough for a bed and chair and hot plate. But she believed in hospitality. Even though she had no table, she invited a couple from her church family for dinner. While the two sat on the bed and she on the chair, she served dinner—complete and delicious and all done on her hot plate.

Since Ruth's dinner party, I've believed that there is no space too small to allow friendship and Christian community to happen.

After a Scrabble Marathon in our apartment, a single told me, "I've never done any entertaining. Perhaps I've been waiting to get married and have a home and the trappings before I got involved. But I think the time has come." She explained that she was telling me about it so that if she chickened out, I would remind her of her obligation and hold her accountable.

Her first party was a great success. Once a church catches on to the excitement of laughing together, the enthusiasm for body life multiplies. And some of that enthusiasm will be life changing.

"I met a lot of people tonight," a guest told Jack. "I talked in depth with several of them. For the first time, I'm sure I would be missed at church if I didn't show up next Sunday."

I had a friend in college who shared that, "I always feel a little guilty when I have too much fun. Somehow, it doesn't seem quite Christian."

That's sad. A party can be a gift from God. It can be the refresher that makes it possible for us to go out and try again. There have been times when I've been so dead, so washed out, that I would have dropped if I had had the energy to fall. Sometimes what I needed was two consecutive nights of eight hours' sleep. Other times it was the soul of me that was tired. Those times what I needed was an opportunity to laugh.

Parties can be very Christian times!

COME AS YOU AREN'T

Goal: To encourage Christians to expand their creativity—visually and vocally.

Basic idea: This is a costume party—the type of costume will be determined by the type of party you choose. Each guest or couple must be prepared to give a two-to-four-minute reading that explains or expands the costumes.

Look at the double objective again. Visually and vocally: When people begin to expand in those areas, they are also expanding their potential for use in creative church worship services. I like the idea of creative Christians— Christians who reflect a bit of the creative perfection of the Creator. And too often we just don't have the opportunity to see his reflection in dramatic ways. Very little in life demands our creativity.

Sunday after Sunday, we have many of the same laypeople help in our worship services. They are the best speakers and the best readers. Or maybe they're the ones we've heard most often—the ones who have had the most opportunity to practice these talents.

Come As You Aren't is an opportunity for a fun party, and a chance to discover new talent to use for God. When someone dares to speak aloud at a party and does a good job of it, she might also be willing to read a poem on Sunday morning that fits with the worship aim the pastor has established.

A friend told me recently that her pastor in St. Louis once dressed as King David, and delivered his whole sermon on the Psalms from David's first-person perspective. It made the experiences of the shepherd, outlaw, and king come alive in a new way. She was so excited about the effect the costume had on the congregation that she talked the pastor into giving the sermon again on a child's level in Children's Church.

One little boy's mother called the week after her son had heard the David-clad minister. "What are you doing at your church?" she asked. "My little boy is totally convinced that a Bible character came to life and talked on Sunday. He can't wait for next Sunday."

I wish our costume party had been held a little closer to St. Louis. I'd have invited that pastor to the party. I'd have asked him to help us spot other hidden talent, people who have never been asked to participate in our church service because we never thought of them, and more important, people who have gained enough confidence in their creative skills to say yes the next time they are asked to praise God with them.

COSTUME PARTY DIRECTIONS

Here are some costume theme ideas:

Famous pair—this makes an interesting Valentine idea, and this is the one we chose.

Famous book character—especially good if you'll be inviting a lot of college students.

Biblical characters—we had two famous pairs come as biblical characters, so the different ideas do overlap.

Childhood heroes or nursery rhyme characters—enter Superman!

Costumes from a specific historic period.

We gave several examples of costumes people might use. This helps get their ideas flowing, and it also tells them that this is not a totally sophisticated party. How in the world would any pair come as mashed potatoes and gravy? No one picked up that challenge, but our friends, the Weynas, came as an egg and bacon. And their costumes were terrific.

Jack and I went around and around on our costumes. It made the pre-party fun, and we never dreamed we could have come up with so many great— though mostly unworkable—ideas. For example, we talked about being the yellow pages and fingers—playing on the ad, "Let your fingers do the walking through the yellow pages." I could come up with a dress made from the yellow pages of an old directory. Jack could get a pair of long johns that we would paint. His body would be the partial fist and his legs could be the two fingers walking. What fun! We finally settled on butler and maid costumes—type casting for our roles that evening.

Costume Party Directions

INVITATION IDEA

Your invitation will have to change to suit the type of party you pick. Here's the way ours read:

Come as You Aren't

VALENTINE COSTUME PARTY

Time:
Place:

Arise and be doing
With costumes ensuing
A night planned for wooing

Occasion—Valentining!
All Cupid's arrows shining
A night with silver lining

Great couples symbolizing
In costumed look devising
A night of love arising

Come as a famous pair!
Bring along a 2-to-4-minute
reading about your pair.

Pair examples:
Romeo and Juliet—
read a bit from the play
Abraham and Sarah—
do a dialogue based on
the Bible story
Mashed Potatoes and Gravy—
Do a reading
from Betty Crocker

WHO TO INVITE

This is a very demanding party, and we invited people we thought would enjoy the challenge. We began with several couples who are life-of-the-party people. We knew they would help carry the evening and make everyone less self-conscious because they would be so free and self-assured.

To this we added a number of people we thought might enjoy this type of party. If we were wrong, they could always RSVP with, "Sorry, but that's the evening we always do the washing." In a way, it's these people who make the party special. When they get excited and share, it's as though the lights flash, and we yell, "Discovered! New talent! How can that talent be channeled for Christ?"

Recently I was asked to put together a choral reading for Sunday worship, and all the people I asked agreed to participate. We even had a practice session. But twenty-four hours before the service, the people began backing out. I was new at the church and had involved everyone I knew. I learned that when friends fail—you ask total strangers! I called Robert and Alice. They said yes, and what a job they did! Later he told me how pleased they were with this opportunity. "I have always been afraid to get up in front of people. That's silly, so I've been taking a speech course. I was praying for an opportunity to test how much I was learning."

Funny how God sometimes lets us stumble on people he needs!

Be open to the possibilities. Maybe at your Come As You Aren't Party, God will allow you to stumble across people he wants to use creatively in your church.

READINGS FOR PAIRS

Since these readings are short, people usually enjoy them rather than panic over them. One couple, for example, brought along a record and pantomimed their Sesame Street characters' voices as the record played. Others came as Two Peas in a Pod. They read directly from the encyclopedia, and were very clever in emphasizing certain portions so the reading was actually hilarious. (Did you know that several hundred years ago, it was considered very poor taste to eat peas in a public place?) Samson and Delilah read from a children's story book, and Delilah actually cut Samson's hair as part of her reading.

Jack and I couldn't find anything on a butler and maid, so we developed the following sequence.

Jack:　　The stage lights grow dim.
　　　　　Drama's plans are laid.
　　　　　The Master's been shot;
　　　　　It's the butler or maid.

Marlene: Tiptoeing through time
　　　　　We're unaware
　　　　　That history's not made
　　　　　Without them there.

Jack:　　Who cut the apple
　　　　　On which Eve fed?
　　　　　Who gave Jael the nail
　　　　　For old Sisera's head?

Both:　　The butler and the maid!

Jack:　　Who opened doors
　　　　　For all Caesar's life?
　　　　　Who cleaned up the mess
　　　　　From friend Brutus' knife?

Both: The butler and the maid.

Jack: Who saddled elephants
For Hannibal's ride?
Who dusted Cleo's face
by Anthony's side?

Both: The butler and the maid.

Marlene: Who steeped the tea
While Luther wrote?
Who made the meals
Bach ate with his notes?

Jack: Who knows their names—
Only a few.
There's Hazel and Bunter;
There's me and there's you.

Both: Life's front stage fills
With many an actor,
But the maid and butler
Are its one stable factor.

A COSTUME VOTE

Ask all guests to rate the other guests'
costumes and readings. You may want
to use ballots like this.

VOTE FOR SECOND BEST

We know that your costume is
obviously the best one here. No
doubt! So we would like you to
vote for the second best:
1. Second best total costume: _____
2. Second funniest costume: _____
3. Second best reading: _____

Just hearing that they have won will
probably be award enough for the lucky
couple. But you might want to go a bit
further.

Adjust your prizes to the type of party
you have chosen. For example, we had
a Valentine Party, so we gave boxes of
valentine candy. To the Second Best
Total Costume, we, the butler and the
maid, awarded a free dinner at our
favorite restaurant—with us along, of
course. This gives us an opportunity
to get to know another couple from the
party even better.

If you are doing famous book
characters, you might award famous
paperbacks or new Christian books that
you're sure most people have not
yet read. If you do biblical characters,
you might give study guides on famous
characters in the Bible. There are
some excellent books on Paul, Abraham,
Moses, Mary, and others.

PRAYER BEFORE THE FOOD

Ask three guests to pray, each
concentrating on a specific aspect of the
evening's fellowship.

Person 1: Thank God for his gift of
creativity

Person 2: Praise God for our voices—to
use in fun and in service for him

Person 3: Thank God for his provision
of food beyond our needs

If you wish, share the following prayers
with those who will be praying. It may
help them focus on what you want to do.
Or you may want to copy these prayers
and have them read. If so, make certain
the reader is in full agreement with what
is said. Do not ask people to share with
God words that ring hollow.

Person 1: Thank God for his gift of creativity

You created the world, God, and all the intricate and enormous parts of it. How can we doubt your creativity when we hear that you never repeat a snowflake design or when we watch an autumn woods put on its coat of many colors? And how can we doubt your creativity when we look around this room? Thanks for the fun of the evening, and for the creative minds you gave us that allow us to play. May I be willing to put as much effort into the more serious creative tasks that you put into my path.

Person 2: Praise God for our voices

Thank you, Lord, that you made us with the power to communicate. Not only can we use an exciting variety of words, but we can give them expression and accent and tone. What fun to have a voice! Thank you for the voices that were part of this evening. And I pray that you will use our voices, and my voice, effectively in the more serious matters on your agenda. May I be as creative when I know you want me to share with my neighbor how I feel about you. May I be as creative when I'm asked to perform tasks in your church. Tonight was easy, Lord, and fun. I'm glad you were here and part of our activities. Tomorrow may not be as easy, Lord. But I want you to know how happy I am that tomorrow you will be there, and part of everything I do.

Person 3: Thank God for his provision of food beyond our needs

Food is very special, Lord, and sometimes I miss that fact as I rattle through predictable thanks. Tonight let me pray with thought. Thank you for the food you've made. Not one of us would starve without it tonight, and perhaps we would never even feel terribly hungry. So it's a special extra from you. How loving of you to provide it for us. Thank you for party foods. What a nice thing for you to give.

FOOD IDEAS
Why not have any great dessert you are good at making?

Or you could follow your party idea straight through the food. For example, in the famous book characters, ask each person to bring a dessert he thinks his character would enjoy. Encourage each person to label the dessert and the character. For example, if someone came as a Hobbit, from *The Lord of the Rings,* he might bring along Hobbit Seed Cakes.

HOBBIT SEED CAKES

1 cup butter
1 1/2 cups sugar
1 can poppy seed filling
4 eggs, separated
1 teaspoon vanilla
1/2 teaspoon nutmeg
1/2 teaspoon cinnamon
1 cup sour cream
2 1/2 cups sifted enriched flour
1 teaspoon baking soda
1 teaspoon salt

Cream butter and sugar until light and fluffy. Add poppy seed filling. Add egg yolks one at a time, beating well after each addition. Blend in vanilla, nutmeg, cinnamon, and sour cream. Sift together flour, soda, and salt. Add to poppy mixture, beating well after each addition. Fold in stiffly beaten egg whites. Pour into greased muffin tins.

Bake in a 350° oven for about 20 minutes or until done. Allow cupcakes to cool about 5 minutes. Remove from tins.

For a Valentine pairs party, all desserts could be either red and/or white. For example, red and white Jello cake.

RED AND WHITE JELLO CAKE

*3 packages (3 ounces each) red flavored Jello
(vary the shades of red by using cherry,
raspberry, black cherry)*
3 cups boiling water
2 cups cold water
1 cup cherry juice
1/4 cup sugar
1 package raspberry Jello
1 cup cold milk
1 teaspoon vanilla
2 cartons whipping cream

Prepare the first three flavors of Jello separately, using 1 cup hot water and 1/2 cup cold water for each. Pour each into a shallow pan and chill overnight.

Mix cherry juice and sugar; heat until sugar dissolves. Remove from heat and dissolve raspberry Jello in hot liquid. Add 1/2 cup cold water. Chill until syrupy.

Combine milk, vanilla, and stiffly whipped cream in a bowl. Blend until mixture forms soft peaks. Fold into syrupy Jello.

Cut the three red shades of Jello into small cubes and fold into the raspberry mixture. Pour into a 9-inch angel food cake pan. Chill 9 hours. Unmold. Spread top and sides with whipped cream and coconut. Decorate with red candy hearts. Serves 14 to 16.

If you have a biblical costume party, you might encourage people to bring recipes that have some Bibleland flavor. When guests arrive, you might serve stuffed dates.

STUFFED DATES

Stuff pitted dates with walnuts, marshmallows, cream cheese, candied fruits, or anything else that sounds like it might make an interesting bite-sized goodie.

Or what could be more appropriate than Heavenly Hash?

HEAVENLY HASH

1/2 pound dates
1 medium can chunk pineapple
1 medium size jar maraschino cherries
1 cup miniature marshmallows
1/2 pint whipped cream

Cut dates into small pieces and mix all ingredients together with the stiffly whipped cream. (Do not use a ready mixed whipped topping.) Sprinkle the top with ground or chopped nuts. Serves 8 to 10.

If you are doing costumes from colonial days, you might consider a blueberry pudding that can be served either hot or cold. Ask guests to bring other desserts.

BLUEBERRY PUDDING

1 quart blueberries
2 cups sugar
3 Tablespoons butter
1/2 teaspoon salt
1/8 teaspoon cinnamon
3/4 cup water
1 loaf bread

Combine blueberries, sugar, butter, salt, cinnamon, and water in a saucepan. Bring to a boil and simmer 10 minutes, stirring occasionally. Remove crusts from bread and cut slices into 1-inch squares. Lay half of the bread squares on the bottom of a 9-inch square serving dish. Pour half the hot blueberry mixture over the bread. Repeat process with remaining bread squares and blueberry mixture. Chill for two hours. Serve plain or with whipped cream. Serves 8.

SCRABBLE MARATHON

Goal: Church and non-church people will be randomly matched in game situation, giving them opportunities to get acquainted.

Basic idea: Couples will combine their Scrabble skills to get the highest score. Each game is twenty minutes long; three games complete the marathon.

You will need one Scrabble game for each four people attending. When I sent out my invitations, I did it in groups of four so I would end up with an even number of players for a complete game.

Develop clever ways to mix up sets of couples for games. Husbands and wives will play as a team. (You can include singles here, but let them know they will have to pair up for the three Scrabble games.)

For example, you decide that the first couple to arrive will play the fourth to arrive. You don't know who those people will be, so it's a rather fun chance thing! Make sure people know how they were chosen to be together that first game.

For the second, you could have the couples whose combined ages are closest play each other. Allow ten minutes between games for couples to complete the higher mathematics!

For the third game, people could play with a couple with whom they share some common number—married the same number of years, same number of children, same number of years until mortgage is paid—whatever they discover.

Set a timer when each twenty-minute game starts. When it goes off, the person playing may put down his final word, and at that point the game is ended. Only the earned score is counted. Letters left are not subtracted.

Make certain couples know that the higher their added scores at the end of twenty minutes, the better their chance of winning. It is to their advantage to move quickly.

Throughout the three games each couple keeps its own score.

To add interest, we also gave each couple this scoring card.

48

INVITATION IDEA

S ure, it's a party

C ome to our house

R ound 7:30 P.M. on (date)

A nd
B e prepared!

B ecause we're gonna play

L ots of Scrabble

E very game for prizes and fun

RSVP

SCRABBLE MARATHON

Names: _____
1. *Combined score—game one* _____
2. *Combined score—game two* _____
3. *Combined score—game three* ___
   Total score: _____
Both pairs in your game should agree on the following items before they are recorded on both your score cards.
1. *Game one—the longest word:* _____
                    person scoring it: _____
(The final version is the one that counts. For example, if someone just adds an "s" to make piglet piglets, *the person who adds the "s" gets the longest word score. If there are two longest words, the word worth the most points wins. Still the same? Toss a coin.)*
2. *Game two—funniest word:* _____
                    person scoring it: _____
3. *Game three: most unusual word:* _____
                    person scoring it: _____

After the games have ended, choose two judges to determine the winners. In the last two categories, the decision will be totally up to the judges.

At our Scrabble party, we gave silly prizes just in keeping with the fun of the evening. You can probably top our humor, but just to get you started, here's what we did.

1. For the highest score, we gave a tape measure.
2. For the longest word, we gave the world's longest pickle. (Actually, this was a restaurant-sized jar of sweet pickle slices.)
3. For the funniest word, we gave a great joke book.
4. For the most unusual word, we gave a terrible reproduction of an abstract painting.

THE PEOPLE MIX

For several reasons, we chose the Scrabble Marathon as a party to mix our friends who are excited about God and church with those who are not. It's healthy for each group to know what the other is thinking. What is our church's reputation in the community? How can we as church people become more involved with the concerns of people who are not with us each Sunday? Both groups have a lot to share, and very few opportunities to do so. The game is common territory. Nearly everyone can play Scrabble. Game-related conversation is easy. "I can't do a thing with five e's." "Does anyone know how to spell dittos plural?" "Who knows a 'q' word that doesn't need a u?"

Second, the marathon angle allows couples to move around a lot, and actually to spend twenty minutes with three other couples. The marathon is pretty much confined to an hour, so after the games people can regroup and conversation can continue for real. Because they have had the mutual game experience, they have some common conversational starting point.

In a way, this party is dangerous. You've heard that religion and politics should be off-limit issues at social occasions. I disagree, but even if I didn't, I have some friends who are so excited about what God's doing in their lives that it just spills over naturally.

When people share what is important to them, great things can happen. For example, a neighbor asks a church member about one of the outreach programs of the church and why people are willing to put so much time and money into it. The conversation turns to God. There is no polemic involved. Two people are talking naturally, the one sharing what Christ was doing through people who serve him, and the other sharing his ideas and observations about this project and the church.

People meeting so they can learn to care about each other! Philip, recently separated, was one of the singles at a marathon. About halfway through the evening, Jack noticed that Philip and Paul, another guest, were missing. Paul later explained, "He told me that this was the first time he'd been anywhere since the separation, and he wanted to bolt. I'm probably the only guy here who has been through a similar experience. We walked around the block several times, and he talked it all out."

A very serious thing to happen at a party. And absolutely right.

DESSERT IDEAS
FOR SCRABBLE MARATHON
Jack suggested alphabet soup, but for what it has in cleverness, it lacks in dessert flare!

You could make sheet cakes, cut them in strips, and position the strips to form letters. Ice the large letters.

CHOCOLATE ROLL

5 egg yolks
1 cup powdered sugar
3 Tablespoons cocoa
5 egg whites
whipped cream
thin chocolate sauce

Beat egg yolks until thick. Add sugar and beat thoroughly. Add cocoa, fold in stiffly beaten egg whites. Spread on buttered, floured cookie sheet and bake about 15 minutes in a 350° oven.

Turn out on floured cloth. Cover with a damp cloth. When cool, spread with whipped cream and roll. Serve slices with chocolate sauce. Serves 8.

AMBROSIA FLUFF PIE

1 package (3¹/4 ounce) vanilla pudding
  and pie filling
1 package (3 ounce) orange-banana flavored
  gelatin
2¹/2 cups water
prepared whipped topping mix
1 unbaked coconut crust

Combine pie filling mix, gelatin, and water in a saucepan. Cook over medium heat. Stir until mixture comes to a full boil and is thick and clear. Remove from heat. Chill until mixture begins to set.

Prepare whipped topping mix as directed on the package. Thoroughly blend into the chilled pudding mixture. Spoon into unbaked coconut crust.

Chill until firm (at least three hours). Garnish with a large puff of whipped topping and a sunburst arrangement of orange sections. Serves 8.

CHOCOLATE MERINGUE PIE

Filling:
1 cup sugar
1/4 cup cornstarch
1/4 teaspoon salt
4 Tablespoons butter
3 ounces unsweetened chocolate
1 1/2 cup warm water
3 eggs, beaten
grated peel of 1 lemon or orange or 1 teaspoon
　vanilla

Meringue:
4 egg whites
1/2 teaspoon cream of tartar
6 Tablespoons confectioner's sugar
1 teaspoon vanilla

8-inch pie crust

Mix 1 cup sugar, cornstarch, and salt. Set aside.

Melt butter in a heavy three-quart saucepan over a low heat. Add chocolate, stirring to melt. Remove from heat. Stir in water and sugar mixture; then stir in eggs. Stir over low heat for about 15 minutes, until slightly thickened and smooth. Stir in lemon peel (orange or vanilla). Cook, stirring occasionally.

Pour into cooled pie crust (8-inch baked crust or crushed chocolate cookie, gingersnap, or graham cracker crust).

For the meringue, beat egg whites until frothy. Add cream of tartar and continue beating until you have soft peaks. Beat in sugar, one Tablespoon at a time. Do not overbeat. Whites should stand in peaks, but should not be stiff. Add vanilla.

Spread in a decorative design over the chocolate and bake 10 to 15 minutes at 350° until peaks are slightly browned.

Cool the pie and refrigerate. Filling will set to firmness as pie is chilled.

FUNNYCAKE

You've heard of Pennsylvania Dutch shoofly pies with the gooey bottoms. This recipe is adapted from that. It consists of a sauce baked in a pie shell and topped with cake.

In this cake, develop your own sauce ideas. Why not try apricot jelly or butterscotch or blueberry or . . . . Here's a recipe built around a chocolate base.
9-inch pie crust with high fluted edges
Chocolate syrup:
3/4 cup granulated sugar
1/2 cup cocoa
3/4 cup water
1 Jiffy white cake mix
Prick bottom and sides of pie crust. Bake in 400° oven for 12 to 13 minutes. Cool. Reduce temperature to 375°.

Syrup: combine sugar, cocoa, and water. Boil about 10 minutes or until slightly thickened. Cool.

Prepare white cake according to package directions. Pour chocolate mixture into the pie shells. Pour the cake batter over the chocolate. Bake for 35 minutes at 375°. Serve topped with whipped cream or ice cream, if desired.

HAY THERE
Goal: To work with two other couples (singles) in the party planning. (You may want to pick people who have not been as involved in church hospitality as you have. In a discipling relationship, you will be sharing what you have learned from your experience.

To invite three different sets of church friends and mix them.

INVITATION SUGGESTION

HAY THERE

Gallop over to (place) on (date), and climb
* into the hay wagon.*
Giddy-up time (time)
Sing 'til you're "horse"
Race around plenty
Trough provided
Whoa: Bring (cost). We've got a high horse!

Basic idea: Plan a hayride and "hay" activities to follow the ride.

WORKING TOGETHER

Pick couples or singles who are interested in helping the church grow together. Perhaps they have never organized an event like this, but they have dropped clues indicating they might be willing to try. Good clues: "I would like to do something like your last party someday." Or, "When I finally get my act together, I'm going to have you over to my place."

Each partner in the Hay There party is responsible for inviting an equal number of people. When I worked with two girl friends on a party like this, we each invited ten, limiting the size of the party to the limitations of the facilities.

Each of us chose people from our small circle of special friends. In a way, we were sharing circles, and in doing so enlarging each circle. As we worked together the party became so much more than it could have ever been with one of us working alone.

HAY RIDE

Now before you yell that a hayride is impossible, remember that I live near Chicago. In fact, I've lived in Providence, Rhode Island, and Lancaster, Pennsylvania, and in each of these cities, it was possible to have a hayride. Look in the yellow pages. You'll be surprised! And if you divide the cost among all those who will attend, the evening can be an event without a mortgage!

Most places that have hayrides also have a barn or large garage for activities after the ride. So plan a total evening.

ON THE WAGON: SOME ACTIVITY IDEAS

Sing
Start with songs everyone knows and just sing through the bunch. Ask someone who plays the guitar to bring it along. A harmonica would be a great addition. Ask an enthusiastic person with a strong voice to take the lead.
Ban all transistor radios!

Joke
Start a can-you-top-this-? joke session. But only if you really know your people! Someone who thinks the wrong joke is just hysterical can change the tone of the party and ruin the evening.

Share
If the group is small or has been divided into several wagons, things will get more "groupy." You might suggest couples share how they met and singles share a bit about their first or funniest date. Hayrides can be romantic.

Constellations
Bring along a constellation book. As a group, pick out the ones in your sky. Bone up on the mythical stories behind them and share with the group.
Or select your own groups of stars, name your original constellation, and make up a story to go with it.

OFF THE WAGON: PARTY ACTIVITIES FOR A BARN, GARAGE, BASEMENT

Barn activities will depend on the makeup of your group. Pick from these suggestions and add your own ideas.

54

Hay There

Folk Games

These are great exercise, and if you have an area big enough, they are a perfect end activity for a Hay There evening. Jack and I and two other couples invited a caller to one of our parties. We told him that few of us knew anything about folk games or square dancing. He was great. He brought with him his record player and a microphone, and in a few minutes we knew enough to skip and twirl following his commands. Most of us were pretty awful, but we got a great work out.

Caller fees run from $25 to $50 dollars for three hours. No one in his right mind would want to jump and prance for longer than that—until he's had years to get into shape.

Be honest with the caller. Tell him this will be a Christian group. Let him know the goals of the party. He might not totally understand, but he will probably respect you for it.

Circle Games

Play some of the circle games you haven't played since you were in summer camp, Youth For Christ Clubs, or 4-H mixers. I'll suggest a few here just to get you tuned back to your past. For additional help, you may want to pump an eighth grader.

In my games, I've changed the traditional names to ones more suited for a Hay There party.

FLYING WAGONS
(Better known as Flying Dutchmen)
Everyone, except one couple, holds hands in a large circle. The excluded couple runs around the outside of the circle, and at any point, hits the hands of another couple. That couple will then run like crazy the opposite direction around the outside of the circle from the original hand-hitting couple. The only object is to get back to the broken space in the line first. The couple who arrives first grabs the hands of the people there, completing the circle once again. The slower couple runs around looking for two other hands to hit. No big deal! But it's fun.

HORSE AROUND
(Better known as Dodge Ball)
Divide the group in half. One half stands in a large circle around the other half. (The large circle does not hold hands.) The object for those in the large outer circle is to hit the legs of the people in the center with a large, soft ball. The people in the center should do their best not to be hit by the ball. When someone in the center is hit, he takes his place in the outside ring and tries to get those who are still left out of the circle. Nasty game! The winner is the final person left in the center. He's probably also in the best condition.

HORSE AND STALL
(Better known as Musical Chairs)
The people are the horses and chairs are the stalls. Place the chairs (stalls) in a circle, one less stall than the number of horses playing. The seats of the stalls should face out. Everyone marches around the stalls in time to the music. When the music stops everyone lunges for a stall. One person will be left without a stall. He's out. Remove another stall,

and keep going until you have one stall and two horses left. The winner is the one to get that last stall. Watch out for some really bloody collisions. I've always felt it was more fair if the person controlling the music could not see the horses.

HORSE AND MULE
(Better known as Ducks and Geese)
Horse and Mule was a sixth grade recess favorite of mine. Regression can be fun. Horses line up on two parallel sides of the building. A mule is in the center. The horses must run from one side to the other. The mule's job is to tag as many of these running horses as possible. When a horse is tagged, he becomes a mule and helps chase the remaining horses. The winner is the last untagged horse.

GALLOP
(Better known as Rhythm)
Everyone sits in a circle, a very wise thing to do if you've just finished playing all those running games. Each person is given a consecutive number—1, 2, 3, and so on. The leader will establish an easy four-beat rhythm. Beat one is measured with everyone slapping his lap. Beat two, everyone claps. Beat three, snap of the right hand; and beat four, snap of the left hand. So the rhythm goes:

Slap
Clap
Snap
Snap

On the Slap, Clap, people should say the word Gal—lop. On the first snap of the right hand, the leader will say his own number. On the second snap, he will say anyone else's number. For example:

Gal
lop
14
2

Number two will then keep in tune with the Gal—lop, his own number 2, and anyone else's number. The object is to stay in time and not get the numbers mixed up. Some people have an awful time with this game. Anyone who messes up with his number or his timing is out of the game. Keep speeding things up until only a few really rhythmic people are left galloping and snapping.

You can make things harder by setting up the chairs in a horseshoe pattern. One end of the horseshoe is the top, the other the bottom. Every time someone misses, he goes to the bottom —instead of being out of the game. Everyone below him moves up a chair and his number changes. The object, of course, is to get and stay at the right end of the horseshoe.

HORSE LAUGH
The object of Horse Laugh is not to laugh. Everyone begins with a straight face. One person is "it." His job is to get the others to laugh by doing anything but touching them. Some people can't go ten seconds before they are howling. As soon as a person laughs, he joins the "it," trying to make all the others laugh. The last to laugh wins!

Relay Games
Relays are easily rediscovered by adults

with straw in their hair. Once again, use those you played when you were a youngster. You may want to change them slightly to make them just perfect for a Hay There party. Here are some examples:

STRAW SAVER
Divide your group into teams. Everyone should find a piece of straw—perhaps off the wagon. Then people line up in team lines and put their straws in their mouths. Place a Lifesaver candy on straw of the first person in each line. When you yell, "Start!" he must pass it on to the next person's straw. No hands allowed. If the Lifesaver is dropped, the person must pick it up with the straw. The first line to get the Lifesaver to the end wins. If lines are short, you may want to make the winner the first line to get the Lifesaver to the back and up front again.

ROOT THE BOOT
Each person in the team should spend time studying the shoes of the other farmers in his group. Then each person should take off both shoes and place them in a pile along with all the shoes from all the other groups. Mix the pile. The first group to find its shoes and have them back on all feet wins. One little thing. No one may find his own shoes. The group must find each other's. And no telling. The team members must be observant.

HOW DOES YOUR GARDEN GROW?
Place a large bag of dried beans as far away from the teams as possible. Give each team a bottle. Once again, teams line up. At the signal, the first member of

each team rushes up to the bean bag and scoops out as many beans as he can—on the back of his hand. He rushes them back to his team's bottle. The object is to get the most beans in the bottle in the shortest amount of time. As soon as one team finishes with all its players, the game is over and the beans should be counted. The team with the most beans wins. It would be possible for the first team done not to have the winning bottle of beans.

WHISTLING FARMER
Teams get into lines again. Place a box of crackers at the far end of the room. The object of the game is for each team member to take turns dashing up to the crackers, eating one, and whistling. He must whistle before he can return to his line and the next person begin. The first line finished munching and whistling wins.

DRESS THE FARMER
For each team, have an outfit of farm clothing—work boots, coveralls, flannel shirt. At the starting signal, the first person in each line must put the clothing on over his own clothes, including buttoning all buttons, and take everything off. Then the second person does the same thing. The first team completely dressed and undressed wins.

FARMERS ALMANAC
Make an identical picture list for each team. Place stacks of magazines at the far end of the room. The first person in each team dashes to find the first item on the list in the magazines. The second finds the second after the first person has

returned with his picture to the line.
If a team doesn't have enough players to
finish the list, people should just go
twice. The first team with a complete list
of pictures wins.

You'll have to adjust your list to the type
of magazines you've got, but here are
some ideas to get you started:

1. A lady the farmer would whistle at
2. A lady the farmer wouldn't whistle at
3. An animal for the farm
4. A money-making crop
5. A replacement for the old horse
6. A five-syllable word the farmer
   doesn't know
7. The farmer's daughter (under ten
   years old)
8. Something the farmer's wife could
   use in the kitchen
9. Something the farmer would have
   no use for
10. Something the farmer would love to
    eat before noon

PRAYER BEFORE REFRESHMENTS
Prayer fits perfectly before the food is
served, but it doesn't have to be limited
to thanks for the food. Encourage people
to thank God for others they have met
tonight, for the fun they are having, and,
of course, for the food. You might ask
people to limit themselves to sentence
prayers and use the pronoun "I" rather
than "we." It makes prayers more
personal. For example, the prayer, "We
thank you for the amazing array of stars,
Lord," becomes "I thank you for the
amazing array of stars, Lord." What a
difference a word can make.

HAY THERE FOOD
Can you have a bonfire? Why not build
the food around it? First thought is
hot dogs and marshmallows, but vary that
a little. Try stick kabobs.

Everyone should find a stick and fill it
with kabob pieces that you have cut
earlier. Kabob pieces can be all sorts of
things. For example:
pieces of hot dog
cut green pepper
water chestnuts
onion chunks
pineapple chunks
Tomatoes get too juicy and fall into the
fire.

VEGETABLE BAGS ON A GRILL
Make individual vegetable packets and
place them on a grill about 1 hour before
eating. Use wide heavy duty foil to make
the bags. Grease the foil well and allow
some butter to melt on top of the
vegetables. In the packets, you could
place:
thin sliced potatoes
carrots
celery stalks
green pepper
onion pieces
cabbage pieces
Add salt and pepper.

BANANA BOAT
For each banana boat, peel one strip
from the banana, keeping the skin intact.
Cut out a wedge of banana. (Use the
wedge as one of your kabob chunks.) In
the hollow put chocolate squares and
marshmallows. Add other things—

cherries, nuts, peanut butter. Cover with the peeled-back banana skin. Wrap in heavy duty foil. Place in coals for several minutes to allow the chocolate and marshmallow to melt.

BARBECUED BEEF

Recipe is developed for ten people. Add multiples to meet the needs of your Hay There party.

3 pounds browned ground beef
2 large onions, grated
1 green pepper, grated
1 large bottle catsup
1 can tomato soup
2 teaspoons sugar
2 Tablespoons dried mustard dissolved in three Tablespoons vinegar
1 1/2 teaspoons meat seasoning
1 celery stalk cut in small pieces

Mix all ingredients and simmer for about 1 1/2 hours.

MOCK ANGEL FOOD

1 loaf white, unsliced bread
1 large can of condensed milk
1 package shredded coconut

Divide loaf into 10 pieces. Dip each piece of bread quickly into condensed milk. Roll in shredded coconut. Stab the slices with the sticks and toast them lightly in the fire.

NEIGHBORHOOD DROP IN

Goal: To meet and talk with neighbors, offering them your friendship.

Basic idea: People who live in close proximity will get together for a short period of time—sharing food and a bit of their lives.

When Jack and I moved into our first apartment, we were so wrapped up in ourselves and the wonderful little world we were creating that we never got around to meeting the lady across the hall. For three months, she was just five steps away from our front door. One night the ambulance came and took her away. We never saw her again.

We didn't even know she was sick. An elderly woman, no doubt she was afraid of us unfriendly, younger people. If we had known—if we had taken the time to know—we could have driven her to the hospital and surrounded her with caring love as she left her familiar surroundings.

The red light on the ambulance wasn't out of sight before Jack and I promised God that we wouldn't repeat our performance. God had placed us in our church, but he had also put us in an apartment building surrounded by people who might need friends.

"Help us to know and love and help the people who move in next," Jack prayed.

PLANNING A
NEIGHBORHOOD DROP IN
Pick a weekday evening—Tuesday or Thursday seemed best for us. This helps to keep the evening casual. On the invitation state the time limits for the drop in. We limited ours to an hour and a half. This announced ahead of time to the older guests that it would not be a late evening, and it told everyone

INVITATION IDEA

We pass you in the hall . . . at mailboxes . . .
   in the laundry room . . . on the steps . . . .
So how about stopping to say hi?

NEIGHBORHOOD DROP IN
7—8:30 on (Date)   (Place)
Bring six cookies

that the evening would be too short to
be tedious.

Hand deliver the invitations. Jack and I
delivered them together. We wanted
both the men and the women to feel
welcome, although we always had many
more women than men at our Drop In
Parties.

Ask people to bring something. We
had our first Drop In around Christmas,
so we asked everyone to bring six
cookies. What a selection we got, but the
cookies were just a means to an end.
When people participate, they feel more
a part of things—a commitment to
make the evening work. They weren't just
coming—they were coming and
bringing. Other things people might
bring would be six pieces of their favorite
candy, three pieces of fruit, six slices
of cheese (you supply fruit and crackers).
Match the season.

Make certain people feel welcome. A
short conversation when you give the
invitation can cover this. One woman
told me, "You don't want me. I've just
moved in and wouldn't have a thing
to talk about to anyone." I named three
other people in the building who had
been there less than a year, and she could
see that I really wanted her to come.
She did.

We had neighbors who never came, but
they were more friendly after our
invitation. It was as though we had
offered a sense of community, and no
one ever completely rejected that.

THOSE AWFUL FIRST MINUTES
No one really knows the others, and
everyone is feeling as though he wished
he had never come. So break the ice.

I provided a pile of construction paper
and straight pins. People were asked
to tear nametags that told something
about themselves.

Some tore and pinned most of their life
history. One lady who lived above us tore
a green leaf and announced that her
name was Fern. Another tore a roller
skate and said that was her favorite
hobby. Jack, always the artist, tore a paint
palette and pinned dabs of all colors to it.

No scissors. This is not an opportunity
for people to demonstrate artistic skill.
It's just a silly little thing to keep people
busy for about three minutes after
they arrive and give them all a common
place from which to start a conversation.

Conversation can be slow at drop-in
parties. You want people to talk, yet many
of them may have nothing more in
common than the block or the building.

Jack and I go over good topics of
conversation before the guests arrive.
Sometimes we even write lists, and when
there's a lag, we remember something we
wrote and ask a question to get things
moving again. Here are some good
questions for us; you'll want to adjust
questions to your own situation.

Who's lived here the longest? What was
the place like when you came?
What do you do for a living? Don't stop
with "I lay tile." Find out what that
involves. What kinds of tile does he lay?
Does he free-lance? Has he ever
worked on any famous buildings?
What was his hardest job?
Where are you going on vacation this
year? Again find out all you can about
that vacation—ever been there before?
Are you driving or flying? How do you

keep the kids happy in the car?

What's it like to be retired? I think the whole thing sounds wonderful, but I'm not sure I would know how to handle my time. Did you prepare for it before the day came?

Where did you live before you came here? Do you have plans for buying a home? What kind of place are you looking for?

How many children do you have? Where do they live? What do they do?

Has anyone seen/read (insert a popular book, movie, TV program)?
Encourage people to share their opinions.

Steer conversation away from any talk about neighbors who aren't at the party. Almost every neighborhood has its strange people—the ones who inspire the most amazing did-you-know? tales. But this type of conversation will ruin the friendliness of the evening. In an apartment, the same thing goes double for talking about the landlord. This isn't the time—even if he or she does deserve it.

We had some amazing things happen at our first neighborhood meeting. We discovered that one of the ladies on the next floor was a retired missionary from India. She had served under the same mission I had served when I was a college short-term missionary. And the woman a few doors over had graduated from the same Christian college I had. She was going through a divorce and was doing a good job of cutting Christians and the church out of her life. The girl across the hall was searching for reality in Christ within her Catholic church. Since her divorce she

felt unaccepted by those who up to that time had guided her spiritual growth.

GOD TALK

I find it easy to talk, but talk about God? That's always been difficult for me. Then I met a Christian who talked about her God as easily as the achievements of her four children. He fit there naturally. I never got the feeling Karen went around looking for places to dot her conversation with things about God, but he was so much a part of her life that she couldn't talk too long without including him.

I can understand that kind of excitement. I'm that way about writing and my job working with Sunday school curriculum. I get excited about writing curriculum and all the wonderful ways of getting teenagers involved in studying the Bible. And sure enough—everyone who knows me knows I feel this way. If she wants to be my friend, she is stuck listening to bits about my job. It's so much a part of me. What made God so different for me? Unless, of course, he wasn't as important to me as my writing —not as much a vital part of my life. I didn't want that to be true.

I began to follow Karen's example of talking about God when he fit into the conversation, rather than skirting around him for fear of embarrassing or turning off the person I was talking with. I just forced myself to be more open about my feelings about my God. I remember one of the first times; I about scared myself to death! I was talking with a seat partner on a plane, and he asked what I did for a living. Previously when I was asked, I would say, "I write curriculum," but this time I told the whole truth—"I write Sunday school curriculum for teenagers."

"Really?" he said. "Isn't that awfully boring?"

"Not for me. I love it. I can point kids toward Christ and a reason for living," I said. "I don't just write curriculum; I believe in what I'm doing."

"That's great," he replied. "I've got a good job, but it's not a reflection of me. I take home the money and that's about all there is to it."

"What do you do?" And we were off discussing his job. My little affirmation of God hadn't cornered him or made him defensive. But God had been there. I had told that man something that was extremely important to me. And I had told him naturally and honestly.

In fact, it was one of the most honest conversations I had ever had. A little later we did come back and talk specifically about how an educated person in this scientific world could believe in God—a difficult conversation that never would have been started if I hadn't dared to fit God talk into my life naturally where it belonged.

That word *naturally* is important. I don't really look for places to inject God, but I try to be aware, with the Holy Spirit's help, of places where he belongs. Then I don't switch topics or be careful —at least, not as often as I used to. Now I just talk him through! And I have never found anyone who was offended by this. Never! Not at Drop In parties or on airplanes or at secular educational conventions!

DO-IT-OURSELVES EVENING

Goal: To work as a team in preparing a total meal.

To carry that sense of community into a do-it-ourselves (inductive) Bible study.

Basic idea: A group of six or seven people will meet to prepare dinner and participate in a do-it-ourselves Bible study. Keep the group small so everyone will fit into your kitchen. Cutting, peeling, stirring together is part of the fun—and necessary for the success of the evening.

THE MEAL

Do nothing ahead of time but gather the ingredients and the pots and pans. When people arrive give everyone an apron and a supper job. We chose to make crepes because they take a while and are a bit unusual. They are not difficult and can be the basis for an entire meal.

Men in the kitchen? For us that's never been a problem. For one thing, Jack loves to cook, so he rules the kitchen. If anything, we've found that men really enjoy trying to master skills that have primarily belonged to their wives.

One evening we had a mini do-it-ourselves party with one other couple. They were planning to be married, and the primary reason they wanted to come to our home was to give Bob exposure to a kitchen. He knew all about TV dinners and fast food goodies, but he had never had the opportunity to learn the real skills necessary to make a stove work for him. We had a great time. Rita and I were in charge of the salad. Jack and Bob attacked the crepes. Jack mixed the crepe

INVITATION IDEA

DO-IT-OURSELVES

Come help us prepare dinner
Slave for hours
Over a hot fire
You'll love it
Come join us in a Do-It-Ourselves Bible Study
Studying the Bible
Discovering what God says
You'll love it
When:
Where:

batter, and did the first few, before turning the task over to Bob. He did perfectly. Rita quipped, "Well, Bob, now you can cook. Let's set the date!"

At a do-it-ourselves evening, you might want to post a list of jobs and recipes involved to get things moving.

For example:

Rita: Wash and cut all the vegetables for the salad

Roger: Make the salad dressing and crepe fillings

Bob: Make crepes

Jack: Mix crepe batter. Supervise main course crepe fillings

Marlene: Make dessert crepe filling

RECIPE SUGGESTIONS

SPINACH A LA *(insert maker's name)*

1 pound fresh spinach
2 celery stalks, diced
3 hard-boiled eggs, chilled, diced
8 radishes, sliced
addition of any other diced vegetables that look interesting
1/2 pound diced bacon
3/4 cup oil
3/4 cup red wine vinegar
2 teaspoons sugar
1 teaspoon salt
1/2 teaspoon dry mustard
1/2 teaspoon pepper
1/2 clove garlic

Remove stems from spinach. Wash leaves carefully; drain. Cook diced bacon until crisp; drain. Put oil, vinegar, sugar, salt, mustard, pepper, garlic in electric blender or covered jar. Blend or shake until well mixed. Toss spinach lightly with dressing. Turn into a large bowl and top with radishes, eggs, bacon, celery, etc.

BASIC CREPE RECIPE

This recipe is used by the Magic Pan restaurant that specializes in crepes.

MAGIC PAN BASIC CREPE RECIPE
3 eggs
1 cup all-purpose flour, unsifted
1/8 teaspoon salt
1 cup milk
1/4 cup water
2 Tablespoons butter or margarine

Put eggs in bowl and beat well with fork. Add flour and salt and continue beating until batter is smooth. Gradually add milk and water, beating until smooth.

Melt butter or margarine and set aside. Before cooking each crepe, brush 8-inch crepe pan with a little butter or margarine. Heat pan over medium heat until just hot, not smoking. For each crepe, pour 2 or 3 Tablespoons of batter into hot pan. Tilt pan from side to side instantly to cover entire bottom of pan with batter. Cook about 1 minute, shaking pan frequently to keep crepe loose. When bottom side is lightly browned, turn with spatula and brown on the other side—about 30 seconds.

When crepes come out of the pan, stack on top of each other and cover with a towel to keep moist and pliable. Yields 12 to 14 crepes.

We have a special crepe pan called "The Crepe Maker." The pan is fun to have, although any small, slope-sided heavy skillet will be fine.

There are a number of basic batter recipes. "The Crepe Maker" suggests this one for 16 to 20 crepes:

THE CREPE MAKER BASIC BATTER

2 fresh eggs
1 cup milk
1 cup flour (all purpose, presifted)
1 Tablespoon soft butter (melted)
pinch of salt

In a mixing bowl, beat the eggs and add milk. Add the flour gradually, stirring constantly with a whisk until the batter is smooth. Add butter and salt and mix until the batter is as smooth as cream. If possible, refrigerate 24 hours before use.

Crepes can be filled with just about anything. Here we make some main course and dessert suggestions, but after you've made several dinners of crepes, branch out on your own with amazing, delicious original ideas.

CHICKEN A LA (Insert maker's name)

1 pound mushrooms, chopped
2 Tablespoons grated onion
2/3 cup butter
6 Tablespoons cornstarch
2 teaspoons salt
1/2 teaspoon white pepper
1 cup half-and-half
2 cups whipping cream
4 cups diced cooked chicken
1 cup chopped walnuts

Sauté mushrooms and onions in butter. Blend in cornstarch, salt, and pepper. Add half-and-half, cream; cook, stirring until thickened. Add chicken and heat to boiling, stirring occasionally. Stir in nuts. Remove from heat. Spoon some of the chicken mixture on the center of each crepe. Fold two opposite sides over the filling. You'll have enough filling for 16 crepes.

ALMOND DESSERT CREPES

To make the filling for 8 to 10 dessert crepes:
1 cup sugar
1/4 cup flour
1 cup milk
3 eggs
1/2 cup chopped almonds
3 Tablespoons butter
2 teaspoons vanilla
1/4 teaspoon almond extract

Combine sugar and flour and add to the milk. Cook, stirring until thickened and bubbly. Beat eggs slightly and add them a little at a time to the milk mixture. Cook until boiling. Remove from heat. Beat until smooth. Stir in chopped almonds, butter, vanilla, almond extract. Cover with wax paper and cool.

When cool spoon into the center of the crepe and fold over the sides or roll the crepe. Top with cherry sauce.

Cherry Sauce:
We use the prepared cherry pie filling and add a dash of nutmeg or cinnamon. Add lemon juice if the filling is too thick.

Crepes are quite filling. You might want to save dessert until after the do-it-ourselves Bible study.

DO-IT-OURSELVES BIBLE STUDY

Objective: Everyone will participate in a depth study of a small passage of Scripture and gain a working knowledge of simple inductive Bible study.

Basic idea: Working in small groups, people will study the Bible for themselves and develop guidelines and principles for Christian living as they work.

Do-It-Ourselves Evening

In do-it-ourselves Bible study, the groups will go through the process many preachers do. First, they will become familiar with the content. Then they will look within the passage to decide exactly what it says—not what they think it ought to say or have heard someone else say it says. Their findings must be based on what is directly stated or indirectly implied in the passage. Groups will then share what they have found and end the study with prayer.

Follow this process. As much as possible, make certain each person has a copy of the same version of the Scripture passage. I've sometimes made photo copies of small passages I want people to study. When everyone has the same words in front of him, long discussions over which word is really the most effective are eliminated.

Choose a short section of Scripture. A good one to try is John 3:16, 17, especially if your guests are really familiar with the Bible but have never participated in an inductive Bible study. They are often amazed by the amount of material they have missed in these two verses. Or you might try Peter's declaration about Jesus in Mark 8:27-31.

Share with your guests a short secular story about inductive study in biology. This will make it easier for them to see what they will be doing in inductive Bible study.

The following story by Samuel H. Scudder is condensed from *Every Saturday,* April 4, 1874.

In the Laboratory with Agassiz
It was more than fifteen years ago that I entered the laboratory of Professor Agassiz, and told him I had enrolled my name in the scientific school as a student of natural history.

"When do you wish to begin?" he asked. "Now," I replied.

"Very well," he took from a shelf a huge jar of specimens in yellow alcohol.

"Take this fish," said he, "and look at it: we call it Haemulon; by and by I will ask you what you have seen."

In ten minutes I had seen all that could be seen in that fish, and started in search of the professor, who had, however, left the museum . . . .I returned to my fish. Half an hour passed, an hour, another hour; the fish began to look loathsome. I turned it over and around; looked it in the face—ghastly; from behind, beneath, above, sideways, at a three-quarter view—just as ghastly . . . .

I might not use a magnifying glass; instruments of all kinds were interdicted. My two hands, my two eyes, and the fish; it seemed a most limited field.

. . .At last a happy thought struck me—I would draw the fish; and now with surprise I began to discover new features in the creature. Just then the professor returned.

"That is right," said he, "a pencil is one of the best eyes."

With these encouraging words he added, "Well, what is it like?"

He listened attentively to my brief rehearsal . . . .When I had finished, he waited as if expecting more, and then, with an air of disappointment, "You have not looked very carefully. Why," he continued, more earnestly, "you haven't seen one of the most conspicuous features of the animal, which is as plainly before your eyes as the fish itself; look again, look again!" And he left me to my misery.

I was piqued; I was mortified. Still more of that wretched fish! But now I set myself to my task with a will, and discovered one new thing after another . . .

The next morning I was able to ask, "Do you perhaps mean that the fish has symmetrical sides with paired organs?"

He was thoroughly pleased. "Of course, of course!"

I ventured to ask what I should do next. "O, look at your fish!" . . .

So for three long days, he placed that fish before my eyes, forbidding me to look at anything else, or to use any artificial aid. "Look, look, look," was his repeated injunction.

This lesson's influence has extended to the details of every subsequent study; a legacy the professor has left to me, as he left it to many others; of inestimable value, which we could not buy, with which we cannot part.

Explain that Bible study is a lot more fun than studying the dead fish, but the look, look, look principle is the same. In order to do effective looking, each person is to assume that this passage is the only one with which he is familiar. (This will help limit discussion to the passage under consideration.)

Ask each person to read the passage three times. They may feel this is unnecessary—after all, they may know the passage by heart. But insist. I've got a fun thing I sometimes do when I'm leading simple inductive Bible study. I

suggest that they read the passage as if they were three different people.

Person 1: Read as if you were a newspaper reporter looking for something to report in your paper.

Person 2: Read as if you were an atheist looking for things to criticize.

Person 3: Read as if you were on a desert island and had never read any Scripture before. Suddenly you see a bottle floating in on the tide. You grab it and inside is today's Scripture. What things could you know about the Bible from this tiny excerpt?

Divide the larger group of six into groups of two or three. I like this because it forces a type of accountability that can be wholesome. Each group will be working on the same passage, and when they compare at the end of the looking-studying time, they can see just how much they missed. So two good groups can double the benefits of do-it-ourselves Bible study.

Ask each group to pick a leader-recorder to write observations they find in their study. Observations are things that are found in the text or things that can be assumed from the text. Encourage people to try to diagram content, look for relationships between different people —any type of creative search which will help them own the Scripture they are studying.

I have found it helpful to give a few observations from this nursery rhyme, if people are unfamiliar with inductive study. It gives them a humorous sample to follow.

Mary had a little lamb.
Its fleece was white as snow.

From this I can state the obvious, and I can look for what I can assume in those two lines. I might suggest, for example:

Mary was probably a girl. Most people with the name of Mary are girls.

She probably lived in a rural area since that's where lamb pets are usually found.

Some lambs aren't white. If they all were, the poet wouldn't have wasted a whole line discussing this unique feature.

Mary probably came from a good home. She seemed to understand how to take care of a pet.

She may have been old enough to understand ownership because the word *had* is used. She owned the lamb. From this we could infer that she accepted the responsibility of the lamb.

Fun? Sure! You're looking for much more significant things in Scripture, but this illustration will help do-it-ourselvers get started. Encourage them to look below the surface. If your guests are from your church, they probably already know the easy-to-find things.

Allow about twenty minutes for this inductive study.

I've done this type of inductive Bible study with high schoolers, and have had the amazing experience of having them protest at the end of the time limit that they weren't finished yet. Could they please have more time! It's exciting to hear young people ask to study Scripture a little longer.

Your groups may do the same thing. But it's a good idea to cut off the group study while everyone is still into it. They have a good feeling about the action of the group, and will want to try again in their private study, or perhaps in their own duplication of a do-it-ourselves party.

Extra Help
If you think your guests won't really know exactly what you want them to do after you've done the above explanation, you might write out these simple directions for them to follow.

1. Write everything you can know or assume from this passage. These questions will help you find things. What do the difficult words mean? What relationships are established here? What laws, principles, teachings are stated or implied? Is there an outline? A progression of thought? Repetition of thought or words? What are the key words or phrases? Why? Key verse? What does each verse mean? If necessary, paraphrase.
2. What title would you give this section to differentiate it from other sections of Scripture?
3. Briefly consider how this section applies to you today. How might you use it in your own life, in your witness to others?

Sample of John 3:16, 17
Stop! Don't read further until you've tried the inductive study of John 3:16, 17 for yourself. Then read the several things I found. This list of observations is very incomplete. But it's a good start.

"For God so loved the world that he gave his only Son, that whoever believes in him should not perish but have eternal life. For God sent the Son into the world, not to condemn the world, but that the world might be saved through him" (RSV).

OBSERVATIONS:
1. I found these attributes of God—he is love, just, all-powerful, eternal.
2. The Son was not personally condemned, because he could save others from condemnation. I can assume the Son was sinless.
3. We must come to God through the Son—no other route.
4. There are a lot of action words —God loved, gave. We believe, receive eternal life. God was not a passive out-there-somewhere God. He was involved.
5. There are some interesting contrasts—God, world; perish, saved; condemned, saved. It's an either-or situation. We can't sit on the fence in our relationship to God's Son.

There's a lot more to find here. It's fun to dig and see what amazing amounts God allowed his writers to communicate with us.

With simple inductive Bible study, I am reminded time and time again that I haven't even mastered the basic content of familiar passages, to say nothing of the principles that I have yet to honestly, consistently implement.

When your Bible study time is up, have groups share the three best things they have found. Encourage free discussion between groups.

We-Can't-Do-It-Ourselves Prayers
End the do-it-ourselves Bible study with we-can't-do-it-ourselves prayers.

Suggest people pray for things that are outside their control. For example, someone might pray for an unsaved friend or family member. Another might bring a missionary's needs to Christ. Still another could share her inability to have a meaningful, regular fellowship time with God.

HAVING WONDERFUL TIME WISH YOU WERE HERE

Goal: To encourage a feeling of family among church members through the sharing of vacation experiences.

Basic idea: Everyone brings ten vacation slides—his best—and shares them with the group. The whole evening will be built around a vacation theme.

I prefer to wait for the middle of winter for this party. By that time, most of us need to remember that there is probably going to be a season of vacations someday again—if we can only wait long enough! (Of course, someone is bound to bring his snow skiing picture, complete with slide of a car adorned with a "Think Snow!" bumper sticker. Forgive him, and let him participate anyway.)

This party doesn't really have a people limit, especially if you have a covered dish supper to which others bring the food.

But most people get tired of slides after about an hour. So plan to adjust your crowd and the speed at which the slides are snapped to fit people's endurance levels. There are projectors that flick automatically every ten seconds—and although I wouldn't recommend using them for this evening, I do like the principle they implement —keep the show moving. One picture

INVITATION IDEA

We'll all come along on your vacation on
  (date, time, place).
Bring ten slides from your best vacation and
  come prepared for the mini-vacation of
  your life.

(OPTIONAL IDEA)
Bring a vacation covered dish—something
  you might have eaten on your most fun
  vacation!
Example:
Seashore trip—fish dish
Southern sun—fruit dish

does not rate a fifteen-paragraph commentary.

Encourage your guests to move their slides quickly. They are just giving a feeling for their days of leisure—not an entire diary account.

SUGGESTED ORDER
FOR THE EVENING

Before guests arrive, make up one "Traveler's Check" for each person.

On each check put a vacation question. Suggest that guests find the answer to that question from as many other people as possible.

While people are getting to know each other better through the Traveler's Check technique, load your slide projector so everything will be ready to go.

I've suggested twenty traveler's check questions. If you have more people, add your own. Remember the object here is simply to give people something to do in the first minutes when guests are arriving. It will spark fellowship—and so will a cup of coffee, punch, and a few hors d'oeuvres.

Traveler's Check Questions
1. Tell me about the worst vacation you've ever had.
2. If you've had a vacation to another country, tell me about some of the cultural shocks you received.
3. If you could vacation anywhere in the world, where would you go and why?
4. If you have ever taken a weekend or mini vacation, tell me where you went and what things you enjoyed most.

5. What's the cheapest vacation ever taken? How did you keep costs down?
6. What things have you done on your vacations with your family that have made the times distinctly "family"?
7. Tell about some interesting people you've met on one of your vacations.
8. What are your plans for this year's vacation?
9. What's the strangest luggage story you've ever heard?
10. If you've ever taken a packaged tour, what advantages and disadvantages did you find?
11. Have you ever had to make an abrupt change in vacation plans and found the change more fun than the original idea? If so, share.
12. If you could take a vacation with your family and anyone else from all of history, what person would you choose and why?
13. What interesting experiences have you had with food in foreign countries?
14. Suppose you couldn't go outside a hundred mile radius of here for vacation. Where would you go and why?
15. What's something you've learned about yourself on vacation?
16. Tell something that happened to you on vacation that was or could have been dangerous.
17. When you travel with your children in the car, what things do you do to keep them from getting bored?

18. Tell a little about your honeymoon trip.
19. What's the best vacation you've ever had and why?
20. Tell about some of the treasures you've picked up on vacation.

After guests have had time to mingle, gather them for the vacation slide show. You might want to do this in two half-hour segments with food in the middle. Another good idea is for you to go first with your vacation slides. Illustrate the speed at which you want guests to move along. The whole success of this part of your party will depend on the pep at which the slides move. Slow slides are deadly!

I once had a slide party that lasted too long, and when the lights went on two men were fast asleep.

FOOD IDEAS
Carry out the vacation idea. If you asked each person to bring a dish that might be served on one of his vacations, you'll have a fine and unusual array of food.

I've found it's a good idea to have a few vacation recipes handy to suggest to people who say, "I can't think of a thing." Once I share a few ideas like those that follow, people usually think of several better ones and don't use my suggestions at all. So use these as stimuli.

Any southern vacation:

ORANGE CUBE GINGER ALE DRINK

2 cups sugar
2 cups water
2 cups orange juice
1/4 cup lemon juice
grated rind of two oranges (optional)
2-3 quarts ginger ale

Boil the sugar and water for 20 minutes. Add all other ingredients and freeze in an ice tray. Pour ginger ale over the orange cubes to serve.

FRUIT COCKTAIL CAKE

1 1/2 cups sugar
2 cups flour
1 teaspoon soda
2 whole eggs
1 can fruit cocktail
1/2 cup brown sugar (optional)
1 cup chopped nuts (optional)

Mix sugar, flour, soda, eggs, and juice from the fruit cocktail. Fold in fruit. Pour all into a greased, floured pan (large). You may want to sprinkle the top with a half cup of brown sugar and a cup of chopped nuts.

Bake until done—about 40 minutes in a 350° oven.

Icing

3/4 cup sugar
1/2 cup condensed milk
1/2 stick butter

Boil all ingredients. While cake is still hot, pierce it with a form and pour the icing over it.

Any mountains or woods vacation:

CHEESE CONES

3 ounce package cream cheese, softened
1/3 cup grated cheese
1/4 cup mayonnaise
parsley flakes

Combine all ingredients. Chill. Shape to resemble pine cones and stick almonds into the cheese base to complete a very realistic looking pine cone. Can be served with fruit and crackers.

Any seashore vacation:

TUNA LOAF

2 eggs
1/2 cup milk
2 cups soft bread crumbs
1/4 cup minced onion
1 Tablespoon minced parsley
1 Tablespoon Worcestershire sauce
1 teaspoon salt
1 teaspoon dry mustard
1/2 teaspoon tarragon
3 cans (6 1/2 or 7 ounces each) tuna,
*   drained*

Combine eggs, milk, bread crumbs, and seasonings in mixing bowl. Beat until blended. Add tuna and mix thoroughly.

Turn into a foil-lined loaf pan. Bake in moderate oven (350°) for about 45 minutes. Lift out of pan; remove foil.

Serve with parsley sauce.

Parsley Sauce
1 can condensed cream of celery soup
1/2 cup milk
2 Tablespoons chopped parsley
1/2 teaspoon dill weed

Combine undiluted soup and milk; stir over low heat until hot. Add parsley to dill weed. This seaside treat will serve about 8.

PRAYER

Before the meal, ask two people to pray thanking God for their vacations and two people to thank him for work that makes vacations possible.

Sample vacation prayer:

Dear Heavenly Father, we all had a wonderful time last summer at the seashore. It seems far away now, but we still benefit from the rest and renewed energy those days gave. I appreciate your gift of vacation!

Sample Work Prayer

I sometimes complain about my job, Lord, especially when I have to get up early in the morning. But then I consider people who don't have jobs, and I realize how fortunate I am. I appreciate your gift of work, Lord. It makes me appreciate the special times of vacation. More importantly, it gives me a way to contribute to others who have needs and to do special things for those I love.

Host Prayer

We welcome your presence tonight, Lord, at our vacation party. Thank you for never taking a vacation from caring and loving us. Thank you for making it possible for us to have vacation foods. Thank you for memories of the nice, quiet days you have given us in the past and for the anticipation of vacations still to come.

VACATION GAMES

If your guests are game people, you may want to plan a few for after the dinner and slides. Actually, let the time of evening and the feeling of the group determine this. For example, if everyone is having a great time talking to one another, don't interrupt with games.

A Visit to China

Play Chinese Checkers. If you don't have enough boards and marbles to plan the game in its original form, play it on a checkerboard. Use ten checkers per player and arrange the board like this:

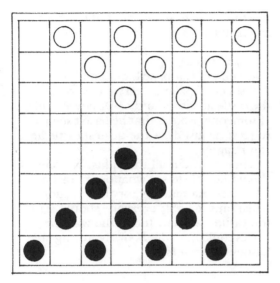

The object is to completely change sides on the board. The red checkers will end up on the same squares as the black checkers started, and vice versa. To do this each player can jump his own and his opponent's checkers. Checkers jumped are not removed from the board. Jumps may be made both forward and backward across the board. The person with his checkers in place first wins.

A Visit to Japan

Jon, Ken, Poi is a quick, easy way to involve everyone. Each person gets a partner. Each partner makes a fist and moves it up and down while saying "Jon, Ken, . . ." On the third word, Poi, each partner makes one of three symbols with his fist. He can symbolize a rock, scissors, or paper. The symbol he makes will determine which partner wins.

scissors—two fingers extended like a scissors from the fist
rock—tight fist
paper—hand open fist

Winners:
Scissors cuts paper, so scissors wins.
Paper covers rock, so paper wins.
Rock breaks scissors, so rock wins.

The person who has made the winning symbol finds another partner and plays again. This continues until two people are left. These two have a play-off. Since everyone playing is reduced by half each time Jon, Ken, Poi is played, the game moves quickly. If both players make the same symbol, they simply do the Jon, Ken, Poi again.

It might be fun to give fortune cookie prizes for this game and also the Chinese Checker games.

I often saw this game being played on the streets of Tokyo. Grown men would Jon, Ken, Poi as a simple way of making decisions. For example, one might say, "I'd love American food tonight." Another would reply, "I'd rather have raw fish." No big deal. Just Jon, Ken, Poi and the winner chooses the food.

Sandcastle at the Seashore

Divide the group into pairs and sponsor a sandcastle building contest. Use clay instead of sand. Set a short time limit and have a judging. Winning pair could take home a toy bucket and shovel prize.

Piñata the Easy Way

Explain that you tried to get a piñata from Mexico, but had to settle instead for some of the goodies that might be in one!

75

Put all these goodies on a tray. Show it to everyone in the room for about twenty-five seconds.

Remove the tray and sing a song everyone knows. Then give people pencil and paper and ask them to list all the things that were on that tray. The person with the longest list wins.

Depending on what's on the tray, you might give its contents as the prize. If people tie, divide the spoils.

The tray might contain just about anything. For example, four different types of candies, a cupcake, a banana, a grape, spoon, napkin, beads, Christian card, pencil, comb, apple, orange, child's storybook, little toys. You'll need quite a

few things to make the game as much fun as possible.

Disneyland Postcard
Everyone gets a pencil and an 8 1/2" x 11" sheet of paper. Everyone is to draw the castle at Disneyland or Disney World. If someone protests that he hasn't seen it, suggest he just draw the neatest castle he can imagine.

Then turn out all the lights. No one should be able to see what he is drawing. Allow several minutes for this creation. Turn on the light; everyone should sign the castle he drew. Judge the winners. Prizes could be comic books featuring any Disney characters.

4

TOUCH ANOTHER GENERATION

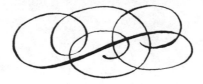

HOW LONG HAS IT BEEN since your church's young people and adults have had a good time together?

The charge has been leveled that the church is the most segregated institution in America—making certain the big people, the little people, and the in-between people never meet. Sunday school classes are age-graded. Many churches have youth and children's church. Teens often sit with their peers during the worship service. Only the youth leaders get to come to youth activities. And my church completed its separation by having a youth prayer meeting. Yes, in many ways being with our age levels is good. For example, I never would have prayed aloud in the adult prayer meeting. But still, I was insulated from the needs, concerns, and joys of my church family adults.

In these intergeneration parties, I would like to see the following things happen:

Parents and young people will be
    provided with a neutral territory in
    which to get to know each other better
    and perhaps like each other better too.
Adults in the church will gain a new
    appreciation for the abilities, talents,
    and gifts of the church's teens.
    Teens will gain a new appreciation
    for the abilities, talents, and gifts of
    the church's adults.
Friendships will be formed between
    young people and adults.

On this last point, often during the adolescent years, it's necessary for the young person to move away from his parents in order to determine who he is and what he believes—as an individual apart from them. During this time, he tends to choose other adult confidants. Hopefully a Christian young person will choose Christian adults from his church—but he won't if he never meets them or has an opportunity to discover that they care about him.

A girl friend of mine attended a church during her adolescent years in which she was totally separated from adults. Her family would part at the car in the morning when they arrived and return after church was over—often not seeing each other in the meantime.

Sara was extremely artistic, but neither of her parents had skills in that area. Her father provided for her physical needs, and her mother tried to keep the lines of communication open, but Sara and she were so very different. So Sara pulled away from her parents and looked for another adult after whom she could pattern her life.

That listening, caring, artistic model that she needed could have come from an adult in her church—if she had known any. She didn't. Instead she chose as her model a non-Christian YWCA leader who taught classes in sketching and oils. Sara slowly drew away from the church. Today she is a model citizen, a perfect example of a community leader. A nicer, more helpful woman you could never wish to meet. She, like her non-Christian teacher, helps other young artists. She is careful not to dampen their enthusiasm. She lets them learn from her by example. She's always excited about their little steps forward. But never a word about Christ. Months go by and she doesn't attend church. God is still a part of her life, but not a very big part. When she was growing up and needed to see how an artistic person like herself could live a life dedicated to

Christ, there was no model available. What a difference a member of her church family could have made!

These party ideas are presented with the prayer that the men and women who implement them will make the Christian difference in the lives of the church children who participate in them.

A word about models. When you get involved with young people, you are putting yourself on display before them. That's dangerous. But perhaps two cautions will lessen the danger.

First, be what you preach. Examine who you are on Sunday. Are you the same on Monday on the job—whether that job is in or outside the home? The answer is rarely an unqualified yes. We're all working daily at better patterning our lives after Christ. None of us has arrived. But the continuous struggle for a greater Christ-likeness should be obvious.

One way I make certain growth is taking place is to ask myself the question, "What is there about me that I wouldn't want the young people in our church to copy?" I take the first answer that pops into my head, and with God's help begin to work on changing that area. For me it's putting products before people. I don't want the young people to copy that in me, and so I am working to make sure that I care as much about the people who work with me daily at my job as I do that the deadlines are met. And the ten or twelve high school people my life touches every week know that this is something I'm working on. I'm working on growing; I'm never full grown.

You might try asking yourself the question, and work on the first area that

comes to your mind. Taking things one at a time makes it easier to measure results, and it's less depressing than trying to tackle the whole less-than-Christlike mess I am at once!

Second, don't be a surface friend. When I was growing up very few adults ever shared their spiritual or personal struggles and problems with me. I wouldn't have been able to handle many of them, but I needed to know that those people hadn't arrived—Christ was still working in their lives. I needed adults to be honest with me.

Perhaps honesty is the key to developing friendships with kids. Share a little of yourself as they are sharing themselves. Let them know that friendship works both ways. You'll listen and care and pray for them, and you expect them to do the same for you. You expect an in-depth friendship to develop.

Jack and I have tried this type of sharing friendship in our senior high class, and with no exceptions found that they were willing to return that friendship. They were willing to participate in making a two-way relationship grow. I recently had iritis, a disease of the iris. My young doctor unthinkingly told me that this was something they knew little about, but it most often happened to arthritic older men. "And," he said, "the worst that could happen to you is that you'll go blind in that eye. Of course, you've got a mild case, and we're going to begin clearing it up immediately."

I was a basket case for several hours after my visit. I kept waiting for my vision to dim and arthritis to set in. (Another doctor later told me that iritis often happens to young women, and for no known reason. Since I'm past the young-woman stage, I was almost flattered by that diagnosis!) The iritis struck Friday and on Sunday I told my class my fears about my eyesight. I shared with them my inability to let God take total control of the problem and to quit worrying. They understood, and we had a prayer time. Three or four of the guys prayed specifically about my eye —prayed with deep concern and without clichés. Right then that small group of teenagers was my support body in the church. I honestly feel that I couldn't have gotten better emotional support and continuing prayer support from any other group in the church.

I feel sorry that so many potential friendships go undiscovered because the church adult and the church young person never have an opportunity to meet and communicate.

What the ideas in this chapter can do is increase your circle of friends. Those friends may be young, but you'll find they will enrich your own personal life —and their participation, creativity, and enthusiasm will increase the quality of life within your church family.

HAPPY BIRTHDAY TO US

Goal: Christian teens and their parents will have an opportunity to share symbolic gifts. This could lead to improved relationships between them.

Basic idea: It's everyone's birthday all at once—one grand celebration for the entire year. Parents will be responsible for making and presenting symbolic gifts to their children; young people will be responsible for symbolically decorating and presenting cakes to their parents.

This party will be most successful if it is sponsored by someone who is already involved with the young people at church —teen advisors, youth pastor, Sunday school teachers. There needs to be a reason why the person giving the party would do so.

Let both parents and teens know what your goals are. You might want to talk about it before the invitations are given. Keep things enthusiastic—after all, this is in part a tongue-in-cheek party.

Be sensitive to the feelings of young people who might not live with a natural parent. Encourage them to bring their guardians. Or there may be some who

INVITATION IDEA

This invitation is written to the young person. Change the wording to appropriately direct a second invitation at the parents.

HAPPY BIRTHDAY PARTY

For your parents!
Don't bring gifts; just bring you!
And don't call and tell us it's
six months 'til birthday time. Everyone
got born some date this year. We just decided
to celebrate all at once
on (date and time)
at (place)

want to come, but both parents are unable to attend. Suggest they pick a parent substitute from the church and come anyway. (Encourage each teen to check with the parents who can't come first. The parents should never feel the church is undermining them.)

Some parents may not be part of the church program. Call these people with a special invitation and perhaps a rundown of the afternoon or evening activities. Parents who refuse to attend something happening at the church may be less hesitant about coming to something in a home or non-church building.

You may be surprised at who shows up for the birthday party.

THE YEARS HERE
(A mixer to get people interacting)
Ask each person to write his age on a slip of paper and drop it into a box—no name necessary. Then each person is to guess the total number of years represented by the group, write it on a slip of paper, and give his guess to you.

Each person gets to ask three people a question from recent history that would help date him. For example, a senior high student might ask me if I remember the bombing of Pearl Harbor. I would have to say, "No, I was too young." That doesn't tell him how old I was, but it gives him a clue. Or someone could ask Jack, "Did you serve in Vietnam?" His answer, "No, but I was in the Army during the war," would begin to date him. Winner is the person who guesses closest to the correct number of years in your box.

The prize could be an inexpensive bottle of wrinkle cream.

SHOW AND TELL
Each family should agree on one funny story about their family that might help the rest of the group get to know them a little better.

To get the thinking started, give an example of what you mean. I might tell the following story from my childhood: My brother Jim went fishing and caught a huge mud carp in the Conestoga River. He knew it couldn't be eaten, but he wanted to show it off to the rest of us, so he brought it home. Unfortunately, mud carp live a long time out of water and my mother can't bear to see something suffer. It was still flopping on our side porch ten minutes after Jim arrived home. Enough. My mother couldn't take it, so she filled the tub with water and in went the fish. That evening every time we made any loud noises the fish would frantically race around the tub. Before morning it had died—of a heart attack, we think. Funny thing. Jim must have gone fishing other times after that, but never again did he bring his catch home

CAKE AND PRESENTS
Divide the parents and young people. During this half hour period, parents will create symbolic gifts for their children, and young people will decorate a birthday cake for their parents.

The cake:

Make several sheet cakes and cut them into large pieces—big enough for three servings—one for each parent and one for the teen. The more decorating materials you can provide the better—candies, food coloring, icing, nuts, candles, construction paper. Each teen's assignment is to create a cake that tells something about how he feels about his parents. For example, Alice could pile a huge icing mound on her cake and later explain to her parents, "I feel a mountain of love for you." Encourage everyone to keep what they do positive and fun. They should know that they will be sharing the symbolism of their decorations with their parents before the whole group.

LEMON PUDDING CAKE

Multiply the recipe to fit your needs:
1 box lemon cake mix
1 Tablespoon finely grated lemon or orange rind
4 eggs
1/2 cup salad oil
1 cup cold water
1 box instant lemon Jello pudding
Mix four minutes until mixture is smooth. Do not over mix. An electric beater is best. Grease pan and dust it with flour before turning batter into it. Bake at 350° for 50 minutes or until done. Cake is done when it springs back in the middle at the touch of a finger and does not leave a finger mark.

BUTTERCREAM FROSTING

4 Tablespoons flour
1 cup milk
Mix into a paste and bring to a boil. Boil until thick. Then cool.
1 cup sugar
1 cup butter
1 teaspoon vanilla
Whip ingredients. Add cooled flour mixture and beat with mixer 7 minutes.

The Presents:
Parents may have more trouble making symbolic gifts than young people have decorating their cakes. So be there with helpful ideas and encouragement.

Supply them with construction paper, scissors, tape, magic markers, material scraps, pins, and anything else that might go into the construction of a symbolic gift. Suggest parents think of some special gift that money can't buy —something they would like to give to their child. You might want to have one symbolic gift prepared ahead of time to give them an idea of what you're talking about.

For example, I might make a gift for Peter, a boy in my Sunday school class. I'd make a great donut-shaped thing. Then I would attach to the circle other more unusual shapes, each with small holes in the center. When I gave it to him I would explain, "Peter, my gift to you is the development of your unusual creativity. Most people choose to go through life predictably. My large donut hole represents them. The other smaller, more unusual and perhaps more difficult shapes represent the directions open to you. You have the potential for doing many creative things for your Lord. My gift includes the prayer that you will dare to do them."

Encourage parents to choose symbolic gifts that can appropriately be shared in front of the whole group.

When both groups have finished, get them together again. You might want to draw family names from a hat to decide who goes in what order. Each young person should share what his cake means and each set of parents what their symbolic gift means.

Be ready to ask parents or teens questions that will force them to elaborate on what they are doing.

PRAYER TIME

When each family group has shared before the group, have a volunteer prayer time.

Keep the prayers optional. If you have non-Christians in your group, this part of the party may be difficult for them. You want them to feel a part of the group—affirmed, not threatened. But to leave out this personal response to God would be wrong. God is a part of the lives of most of the people who will attend this party, and he should be actively included.

People should thank God for other members in their families. Suggest they be as specific as possible. For example, I might pray for Peter, "Thank you, Father, for Peter's creative skills and his willingness to use them for you." Or I might pray for my father, "Thanks for Dad, Lord. I like the way he keeps track of my family history and shares all the interesting facts about my background with me."

CAKE EATING PLUS

Young people should cut their cakes and share with their parents. Add to the cake any other goodies you wish—nuts, ice cream, candy, punch, coffee.

Suggest that people divide into groups of families—two families to each group. While the groups are eating they should be planning a humorous roleplay to present to the entire group after the cake is gone. Suggest that in the roleplays

the teens should play the parents and the parents the teens. Everyone should be included in the roleplay.

Here are some roleplay ideas—enough for ten family units. If you need more, you can use one twice, or better still, develop some original ones.

Roleplay 1

You're in a van on vacation and have been traveling six days without any long stops. Roleplay your conversation. Keep it funny, and somewhat realistic. When you put on your roleplay for the whole group, line up the chairs as if they were van seats.

Roleplay 2

You are the modern version of the Swiss Family Robinson. Off you've gone to live in a tree. Roleplay some of your conversations including some of the fun and hardships of living in a tree. Be funny. When you share your roleplay with the whole group, you might stand in different parts of the room as if you were on different limbs of the tree.

Roleplay 3

You're all zoo animals—some are parent animals and the rest are teen animals. You're all behind the same zoo bars. Hold a conversation about the people watching you. Be funny. For the roleplay in front of the whole group, you might want to line up as if you were all at the bars looking out.

Roleplay 4

You are part of a committee formed to ban chocolate in this country. You are presenting your case to the law-making body. Be funny as you give all the crazy ideas you can on why this makes sense. When you share your roleplay with the groups, you may want to sit in a horseshoe line.

Roleplay 5
You are part of a parent-teen baseball game. Make comments you might make to each other if you were really playing the game. Be as funny as possible as you mime the motions of the game. When you give the roleplay, you may want to stand in a diamond shape as if this room were the playing field.

After the groups have put on their roleplays, consider following the last one with a real parent-teen baseball or volleyball game.

PICTURE PERFECT POLAROID PARTY

Goal: Church people who do not ordinarily have contact with young people will work as team members with them in order to get to know them better.

Basic idea: Adults and teens will participate in a Polaroid camera scavenger hunt.

Invite similar numbers of church adults and young people to the Polaroid Party. With the adult guests, vary the ages. Some might be recently married; others could be grandparent-age. None of the adults invited should be parents of teens.

Make a special effort to let everyone know the goal of the party. This makes everyone slightly responsible for its

success. You might even enlist the help of several teens in planning the adult guest list. Include two or three adults who already have friendship relationships with the young people.

You'll need to collect a Polaroid camera for each group of six guests. If the scavenger hunt teams get much bigger than six, there won't be enough group participation.

PARTY PATTERN
(everything is built around the picture idea):

Give Away a Piece of Yourself
You'll need to do something as guests arrive to break the ice and get teens and adults used to talking to each other. So try this idea. As each guest arrives, take a close-up picture of his face. Cut that picture into four pieces with part of his face on each piece. Explain that he is to give the pieces away to people he doesn't know very well. Teens should give their pieces to adults, and adults should give their pieces to teens.

When they give their picture pieces away, they should allow the person who receives the piece to ask them three questions about themselves. Give a few examples of the type of questions that might be fun. For example, after an adult gives a teen a piece of his picture, the teen might ask. "What do you do for a living?" "What was the most fun party you ever attended as a kid?" "How do you feel about the young people in our church?" Each of these questions demands more than a one-word answer, and that's good for conversation.

A teen might give an adult a piece of

Picture Perfect Polaroid Party

INVITATION IDEA
(In this spot place a Polaroid picture of yourselves or your home)

Time: *(Remember you'll have to have
    daylight)*
Place: *See picture for house (or hosts)*
*Come and team up with someone twice or
    half your age to take the pictures of a
    lifetime!*
Bring one ice cream topping!

his picture, and the adult could ask three questions of him. For example, "What's the most difficult thing about being in school right now?" "What are some of your favorite activities?" "Tell me something about the young people at our church that I probably don't know."

Scavenger Hunt

After the mixer, divide the group into teams for the scavenger hunt. Try to have an equal number of teens and adults to send out on each team. Remember the old-time scavenger hunts when each team was given a list of things to find and bring back to home base first? A Polaroid scavenger hunt is exactly the same thing, but teams are given a list of pictures to bring back instead of a variety of other paraphernalia.

Give each team a camera, instructions on how to use it, film, and a list of the pictures it is to bring back. First team back wins. You may want to have an extra camera on hand in case one doesn't work. A camera failure could spoil this part of the party.

Here's a starter list of pictures. Some of my ideas won't make sense in your area, but you could use this as an idea base.

Polaroid Picture List

1. Everyone in your team in one picture. Photographer may not be anyone attending this party. Photographer's name: _____
2. Anyone standing on a roof.
3. A married couple not at this party holding hands.
4. A red car stopped for a red light.
5. Someone less than a year old.
6. A garage mechanic yelling.

7. A wild flower with a bug on it.
8. Something that doesn't make sense.
9. Someone over sixty, laughing. Person laughing should not be from this group.
10. Someone doing something legal.
11. A father with an elementary child.
12. A green thumb.

Half the fun of the evening will be groups sharing their shots. You might want to make a display board. A long piece of paper—butcher paper or a paper tablecloth—would be perfect.

Make a great production of giving the winners a prize. For example, give each a cheap picture frame for his favorite scavenger hunt shot.

Food

Sundaes are easy and always popular. You supply the ice cream and have the guests bring different toppings. Encourage people to be creative. Here are some more unusual topping suggestions—just in case anyone asks for your ideas.

marshmallow
canned prepared pie fillings
honey and cinnamon
granola
chopped fresh fruit
coconut
butterscotch pudding
sunflower seeds
and all the regular goodies too

Picture games

After the scavenger hunt and some snacks, the party may have gone on long enough. Or people may enjoy working

88

together on some different types of pictures. Keep your ear carefully tuned to the tone of the party. Don't let things drag.

MAKE-A-PICTURE GAME
You're the photographer

From everyone at the party, you will select a different group to plan each crazy picture you suggest. Groups will have sixty seconds to plan and then everyone must stand perfectly frozen while you take the shot. When all the pictures have been taken, the whole group will judge which are best and you'll award prizes.

You'll want to label each shot, so people will remember exactly what was being depicted in the shot.

One key to this game's success is choosing unique groups for each picture. Here are some ideas:

1. Everyone in blue jeans. This means that everyone wearing jeans will be part of this picture. You may have six in the shot or only two. However many are in this category will have to develop the picture you assign to them. A person may fit every category and be in every picture or be in just two or three. That's part of the fun. No one knows which pictures he will be in until you announce the group idea.
2. Everyone who has prepared his Sunday school lesson for this coming Sunday.
3. Everyone wearing purple.
4. Everyone with shoestrings.
5. Everyone who remembers being jealous of a blond.
6. Everyone who can name all our church board members.
7. Everyone who knows the church telephone number by heart.
8. Everyone who would choose a butterscotch sundae over a chocolate one.

Add others. People who fit in these categories will develop the following pictures. Encourage people to be as funny about this as possible.

1. Picture of a farmer in his barnyard. Suppose everyone in blue jeans had to make this picture. One person would be the farmer and the others would be different animals. After the shot is developed, it can be labeled and placed on display. Later it can be judged against the others in some crazy categories.
2. Picture of a cow jumping over the moon.
3. Picture of the California gold rush.
4. Picture of the old woman in the shoe and her family.
5. Picture of a Ripley's Believe It or Not exhibit.
6. Picture of a famous constellation.
7. Picture of a woman's head with rollers in her hair.
8. Picture of a magazine ad for deodorant.

After all these crazy pictures are taken, put them up for judging. Each person gets one vote in each category. Here are several categories you might want to use.

1. Picture that best illustrates the assignment: _____
2. Picture that shows the craziest amount of creativity: _____

3. Picture least likely to ever turn up in our church newsletter: _____
4. Picture with the most creative mix of young people and adults: _____

Since you really won't know how many will win in each category, you'll want to have cheap, expendable prizes. For example, a handful of peanuts to everyone who was in the craziest picture, or a voucher for an ice cream cone at a local store.

If your church has an appropriate bulletin board, you might want to make a display out of these pictures and put them there for the whole congregation to enjoy.

BABY PICTURES
If you can get baby pictures of each guest, display them on a board with a number beside each. Each guest gets a piece of paper, and the object is to tell the name of each baby pictured. The person with the most correct answers on his sheet wins. The prize—how about a jar of baby food?

PICTURE TALES
Before guests arrive, cut interesting pictures from magazines and put them on cards. For example, you could have a picture of a boy riding a bike, a ripe tomato, a mother at a supermarket, a teen playing football, a roast turkey, a couple fighting. The pictures should have no common theme.

Turn all the cards face down in the center of the room. To start, a volunteer will pick up any card, look at the picture, show it to the group, and begin telling a story about it. After about a minute of the story, you yell, "Switch," and that person will stop—even in mid-sentence. He will then point to another person who will pick up another picture and continue the story. Continue this way for several minutes. When one story has gone about far enough, you can start over with the pictures that are still face down. This is a fun, creative, and completely nonsense game!

Here's how one story might start out. The first person picks up a picture of a girl holding roses. He might say, "Ellie was just thrilled. Her first roses. But she had no idea who had sent them. No card. You would think that the person . . ."

And you yell "Switch!" and the person points to the next person to continue the story. She picks up a card of an old mule, and says, " . . .would have been more considerate. After all, she spent every day in the fields working with her old mule, who was actually allergic to roses. In fact, even a whiff of them sent him off kicking and braying. Ellie decided that she must . . ."

And so the game goes on.

STITCH AND CHATTER EVENING
Goal: Junior high girls and the older women in the church will have an opportunity to become friends and share or learn a handicraft skill.
Basic idea: Women with needlework and other craft skills will share them with young girls from their church. They will work together through the evening to teach and learn the basics in that area.

INVITATION IDEA
for the Junior High Girls

*Elizabeth from the TV show "The Waltons": It's great for you
natural cooks to just know that you need to throw in a pinch of
this and a dash of that. But if you don't pass on what you know,
how will I ever learn? I'll go through the rest of my life without
ever being able to make a lemon cake as good as yours.*

*Ever feel like Elizabeth? The older people have so many skills,
and very few get passed on.*

*Come, learn a skill taught by one of the women of our church.
You'll love it!*

When:

Where:

*Instruction available in: (change list to fit the skills of the people
in your church)*

darning, crocheting, macrame, breadmaking, knitting

Of course, this idea could be tried with the teenage boys and the men of the church. In this case, the older men of the church could teach the junior highs some handyman skills. The basic idea would be for men with skills such as woodworking, electrical ability, or mechanical skills to share them with young men.

Let me explain why I suggest fancy work with needlepoint and crocheting for girls and the traditional skills of building and mechanical work for the boys. Very simply, for this party to work, you have to have older adults who are skilled in teaching things. It's easier to find older women to teach needlepoint than woodworking. Many of these people have grown up in a time when the lines between womanly skills and manly skills were clearly drawn. But if you have an older woman who can handle the circular saw or an older man who enjoys tatting, great! Include everyone of the correct age and sex who has something to teach.

This party idea has its conception back in my old junior high days in my Lancaster county neighborhood. The women in about a mile radius decided they would meet once a month to do their mending together. Since I was the only half child/half woman in that area, I was invited to attend. It was great fun. I got to know and appreciate these women, some of them four times my age. The adult conversation was great. I learned some of their concerns and the things that they considered their successes. I learned to talk with them, and was thrilled when they listened and seemed to think that what I said made sense. They made me happy that I would someday be an

adult woman.

Few of these women were strongly involved in a church and many didn't claim to be Christians. Yet because they lived in the same community, they seemed to sense that they should be important parts of each other's lives. I've rarely seen that type of support and caring duplicated by the local church. But perhaps this party will help change that.

Call or see each girl and explain in detail what you have in mind and what your goals for the evening are.

And, of course, before you can send out invitations, you'll need to get the support of all the older women in your church who are willing to be part of your togetherness activity so you'll know what crafts you'll be offering.

Stress to everyone that this is not a big achievement evening. Everyone will be having a good time even if they never master anything as simple as the chain stitch. The big thing is learning to know each other and appreciate each other's abilities and skills.

NO FEAR FACTOR
You may be hesitant about trying this party idea, because you've heard horrible tales about junior highs. A few of them are probably even true, but this party has a few built-in safeguards which will eliminate the discipline problems that can be part of this maturation level.

Junior high girls, usually ages 12 through 14, relate extremely well to the generations older than their parents. So grandparent-and-older-aged women are often on their wavelength.

Junior high girls have rarely been

exposed to traditional handicraft. It's something new, and by its very newness will hold their interest. Their hands are fully developed and they have the mental skills to master patterns quickly. I remember the day my great-aunt Sarah came to visit. I was twelve. I couldn't tell you what she looked like, but I'll never forget the gift she gave me. She taught me to do the chain stitch and two other crochet stitches. I loved them. I think I put edging around every handkerchief in the house. Of course, Kleenex soon became popular, and I discovered dating, so I never really learned skilled crocheting. But in that one day I had my only taste of "grandmothering" and I just loved it. To this day I use the needles she gave me to catch tears in knits, and more importantly, I learned to look with new appreciative eyes at the beautiful things the women of other generations had made.

You're supplying grandmother figures. Our mobile society has robbed many young people of their grand-parents, and our communities often do not have a good mix of older and younger people. Many young people have never even held a conversation with someone who remembers World War I. They have never touched the wrinkled hand of an elderly person and glimpsed a bit of the preciousness of life and how very short life can really be.

With no boys present, junior high girls will not be playing to their most important audience. Discipline problems won't exist. On an evening like this, you'll see reflections of the type of woman these people will be in five years. It can be a very reassuring evening!

With this evening, you are also opening the way for turnabout occasions. At this party the older people are the teachers, but there are many things young people can teach and do for the older people as well. And these things may happen if you provide a friendship opportunity. One local school system started a grand-mother adoption idea and had its junior high young people plan an evening for senior citizens. Thirteen-year-old Billy told me about his elderly date. "I couldn't believe she agreed to come to our party, and was it ever interesting to listen to her talk! She was born and lived for twenty years in England and still has an accent. And she's lived in the same house in Oak Park for fifty-four years. That's a lot longer than even my folks have been alive.

"I don't think she had ever been around young people much before our school party. But now that it's over, I think she feels good about us.

"I brought brownies to the party, and she told me how much she enjoyed them. So I'm planning to make her some more. Maybe that one evening was the start of a real neat friendship.

"She belongs to a senior citizens' group," he continued. "They often make interesting craft projects. She's promised to make me a monkey out of a sock. I've seen them in stores and I think they're kind of neat.

"You should have been at the party. Some of the people there told us stories that went clear back to horse and carriage days. All together they had lived over 2145 years! And if I couldn't learn something from all that experience, I'd have to be pretty dumb."

STRUCTURING THE EVENING

Display
Consider having a little exhibition of the women's work on display when guests arrive. Be sure to place the names of the people beside their handicrafts. In communities where there are fairs, some women may have won ribbons. If so, display them with the crafts.

Preparation
It will make things easier for you if you ask each woman to supply all the materials one girl will need. This would include the correct needles, yarn, thread, anything that the junior high will need to practice. This doesn't mean that the older guests are to bring enough materials for the girl to complete a whole project. Just enough for her to learn on. (If you have more junior highs than older women, some will have to teach two or more girls and should bring supplies for them all.)

When Guests Arrive
Have magic markers or crayons and nametags. Each person should write her name in large, clear letters. She should choose a color that tells something about herself.

She should then talk to several people she doesn't know and find out why they chose the colors they did. In these early moments, you want to establish communication between the older and younger group.

Tour Through the Crafts (Optional)
I like this option because it gives each girl three minutes with every woman at the party and exposes the girl to all the crafts represented.

Position the teachers at different spots throughout the house where they will be working for the evening. Give each teacher a number which she sets by her station. Then ask all the girls to go to different spots so there will be at least one girl with each teacher. (If you have more teens than teachers, two girls may have to go to the same spot.)

Each girl spends three minutes with the first woman. When you blow a whistle, she will move on to the next woman. So the girl at number 1 will go to number 2. The girl who started at number 4 will move on to number 5. If you have only 9 numbers, the girls will move to number 1 after they have been to that last number.

During the three minutes people should find out a little about each other —names, where they live. The teacher might have time to show what she does and tell how she got started.

This is optional. If you have a large group of teachers and junior highs, it would take too long to do this. Simply go from the colored name activity to the actual teaching experience.

Learning a Craft
Each girl should go to the woman to whom she has been assigned. You may want to tell each girl before the party which woman she will be working with. Some women will be more popular and outgoing than others and the girls who get the women who seem less exciting might groan out loud if they don't know who their teacher will be. That would definitely dampen the evening. Also if decisions are made ahead of time, the

girls may have some choice in what they will be studying.

As the couples work around the house, visit the little groups. Give encouragement. If necessary, sit for awhile and enter into the conversation. Tell the workers that they will show what they have completed—obviously not much, but it will allow for group cheering, clapping, and a sense of achievement on the parts of the teacher and student. I remember how I felt when a woman in my neighborhood taught me to color black and white photographs with transparent oils. I took my pictures to our neighborhood meeting, and the women were absolutely amazed at how beautifully I had done. I found those pictures in my attic recently, and they weren't so hot. But that affirmation, I believe, was real. I wasn't good at it yet, but I was doing something they didn't do and they were pleased with my effort!

GRANDMOTHER'S KITCHEN

There are any number of options here. I've suggested just three. But food will be a fun part of this evening no matter which option you choose. Rumor has it that both junior high girls and grandmother-aged women love to eat!

Option 1
Have each grandmother bring along her favorite dessert. Put her name beside her dessert. You might also want to have recipe cards beside the desserts so the young person can take home the how-to and reproduce something she thought was delicious.

Option 2
Grandmother's cookie jar. Ask each guest to bring along six or seven of her favorite cookies. You supply the milk, hot chocolate, and Sanka.

Option 3
Plan an old-fashioned meal—the type that grandmother might have made when she was a girl. This option is by far the most difficult, but if everyone over forty brings something, the evening's expenses won't be significant. Here are a few recipes just to get the old-fashioned part of you thinking!

SPANISH CREAM SALAD

1 1/2 Tablespoons unflavored gelatin
3 cups milk
1/2 cup sugar (scant)
3 egg yolks
1/4 teaspoon salt
1 teaspoon vanilla
3 egg whites, beaten stiff

Mix the cold milk and gelatin. In double boiler, scald. Add sugar and slightly beaten egg yolks.

Return to double boiler and cook until mixture coats a spoon. Stir constantly. Remove from heat, add salt, vanilla, egg whites. Turn into mold. Chill.

Garnish Spanish Cream with orange marmalade.

You may want to make individual molds. If so, use only 1 Tablespoon gelatin. One mold will serve 8. Make as many molds as you'll need for your entire group.

MOTHER'S MEAT LOAF

1^1/$_3$ *cups dry bread crumbs*
2 cups milk
2 pounds ground beef
1 pound ground pork
4 eggs unbeaten
^{1}/$_2$ *cup minced onion*
2 teaspoons salt
2 teaspoons Worcestershire sauce
1 teaspoon sage
1 teaspoon garlic powder
^{1}/$_4$ *teaspoon pepper*

Sauce:
^{1}/$_2$ *cup catsup*
^{1}/$_3$ *cup brown sugar*
2 teaspoons dry mustard
^{1}/$_2$ *teaspoon nutmeg*
^{1}/$_2$ *teaspoon oregano*

Combine bread crumbs with milk; let stand for 5 minutes. Add remaining ingredients; mix thoroughly. Shape mixture into loaf on a 13" x 9" x 2" pan. Mix catsup, brown sugar, mustard, nutmeg and oregano; spread over meat. Bake at 350° for 1½ hours. Serves 16.

CHICKEN CASSEROLE

4 chickens, cooked and deboned
4 packages frozen broccoli
4 cans condensed chicken soup
2 cups mayonnaise
2 teaspoons lemon juice
2 teaspoons curry powder
2 cups bread crumbs
2 cups cheddar cheese, shredded
4 Tablespoons melted butter

Cook broccoli. Line buttered casserole dishes with broccoli. Cover with sauce made of soup, mayonnaise, lemon juice, and curry powder. Place chicken pieces on top. Cover with bread crumbs, shredded cheese, and top with melted butter. Bake 25 minutes in a 350° oven. Serves 16.

CRACKER PUDDING

This old Pennsylvania Dutch recipe is one of my favorites, and I'm not alone. Recently when the company I work for had its hundredth birthday, Cracker Pudding won first prize in its Early American Foods Contest.

4 quarts milk
3 cups rolled saltine crackers (not so fine)
4 scant cups of sugar
2 cups coconut
8 eggs (whites separate)

Blend sugar and egg yolks thoroughly. Pour scalded milk over them and add crackers. Cook but don't boil. When mixture nears the boiling point, add coconut. Heat again to near boiling. Remove from stove and fold in stiffly beaten whites. Cool. Serves 16.

OATMEAL CAKE

1 cup oatmeal
1^1/$_4$ *cups boiling water*
^{1}/$_4$ *pound butter*
1 cup brown sugar
1 cup granulated sugar
2 eggs
1^1/$_3$ *cups flour*
1 teaspoon soda
1 teaspoon vanilla
^{1}/$_2$ *teaspoon cinnamon*
^{1}/$_2$ *teaspoon nutmeg*
1 teaspoon salt

Pour boiling water over 1 cup oatmeal. Set aside and do not stir. Cream butter, brown sugar, and granulated sugar. Add 2 whole eggs one at a time, beating well after each. Beat oatmeal mixture with a spoon and add to creamed mixture. Fold in flour, soda, vanilla, cinnamon, nutmeg, salt. Bake in a long pan at 350° for 25-30 minutes.

Topping
1/4 pound butter
1 cup brown sugar
1 cup coconut
1 cup chopped nuts
2 egg whites, beaten stiff

Mix the butter and brown sugar over low heat until it comes to a full boil. Remove from heat and add coconut, nuts, egg whites. Spread over the cake; return it to oven and bake 15 minutes longer.

It's a good idea to wait until the cake is almost done to make the topping so you can add it to the cake while it's still very hot.

PRAYER TIME
No matter which refreshment direction you go, plan a prayer time before the food. Ask two older women and two younger ones to pray. The older ones should thank God for the girls and the girls should thank God for what the older Christians in their church can teach them. The prayers might go something like this:

Woman Teacher: "It's been an exciting evening, Lord. I'm extremely happy with the young women who are part of our church. Thank you for them, and especially thank you for (girl she worked with), and her potential for serving you. It was fun working with her. I believe I speak for all the women here when I say, 'Thank you, Lord, for our young women.'"

Junior High Girl: "Dear Heavenly Father, I learned a lot tonight and perhaps most important, I gained an appreciation for some of the older women in our church. Thank you for their trust in you. I want to grow toward you, as they have. Thank you for giving them to me as examples and as friends."

5

PROJECT
PARTIES

Three parties that can
spill over into your
church worship service

EACH OF THE PARTIES we've talked about so far have been directed inward—aimed at getting those who attend better acquainted with one another. Now I would like to suggest three party ideas that are directed outward—toward others who see and hear the benefits of the party in the morning worship hour or other all-church functions. At one party the guests will make banners. At another, they will develop a Scripture and slide presentation, and finally they will work at encouraging missions awareness at a party to plan a party.

Each of these ideas has special appeal to teenagers and young adults in the church. Plan to include these groups as you work through the ideas.

When a party is structured around a project, it's easy to determine if the goals were met. If the project got planned, you made it! But with these three ideas, go a step further by aiming at results like the following:

That people of different age groups will work together harmoniously. Each will contribute his best and be willing to assume the roles of leader or follower in order to most effectively complete the project.

Each person in the project will understand the project's greater purpose and accept prayer responsibility for those at whom the project is aimed.

That the total church will benefit from these projects and through them be pointed toward God.

That young people and older adults will accept additional responsibilities for the ongoing work of their church.

That each person will have the opportunity of working with church leaders in brainstorming and creating these ideas.

RAISE THE BANNERS HIGH
A party to make special church banners

Goals: People of different ages will brainstorm, plan, and develop banners for the church. (Quite often it's nice to have a holiday reason for the banners. An Easter service, a youth day program, the Christmas Sunday school program all provide excellent banner opportunities.)

Participants will come to know each other better and, by working on this project, feel more a part of the ongoing activities of the church.

Basic idea: Church people will create colorful and artistic banners to be hung in the church sanctuary or fellowship hall to create a mood of celebration.

I remember my first exposure to making banners. For weeks my pastor had been preaching about God's giving of his Law to the children of Israel. He carefully explained each commandment and its implications for Christians today. Finally the Law had been explained, and he suggested that we plan a celebration as a conclusion to the series. We would be praising God for his loving understanding in setting perfect rules for us to follow. The pastor encouraged us to use our creativity and come with praise banners to decorate the church the following Sunday. It was great. The place was filled with homemade banners praising God and affirming our commitment to his Word. "Praise Our Lawgiver!" "Obey—Yes!" "Wave Our Praises High." What a variety of phrases and designs. Our church was beautiful in a new way, and its uniqueness was an excellent stimulus to worship.

INVITATION IDEA

Plan a word-of-mouth invitation. Select the number of people you want. Let's suppose you think nine people could develop the three banners you are planning. Begin by sharing the idea with the pastor. If he's enthusiastic, continue by asking him to attend the party and explain what direction he is planning for the worship on the Sunday when the banners will be flown. Explain that he is to start the invitation chain by calling one other person he thinks might enjoy this type of activity. That person is to be a different sex and different age than he is. That person's number is 1. After that person accepts, the pastor should explain that the person is to call one other person of a different age and sex and invite that person, and give him the number 2. And so on until nine people have agreed to come. In this way, you'll get an unusual mix of people, and probably each person will have at least two other friends as part of the group. Make certain however that everyone invites another person who in turn accepts. You might want to follow the chain through a second time a few days before the party.

MATERIALS EACH
GROUP WILL NEED

scissors that are sharp enough to cut
  material

white glue, such as Elmer's Glue
marking pens
needle and thread
banner fabric

Heavy fabrics work best because they cut easiest. Felt is most common, but burlap, canvas, and suedecloth will also work.

Trimming material: Here you are limited only by your supplies and imagination. Consider ribbons, fringe, artificial flowers, pictures large enough to be seen throughout the church.

Optional: Patterns for letters. Everything else works well drawn freehand, but your people may prefer stencils for letters. The larger the better. Check your local artist supply store. If you're operating on a huge budget, you might consider professional letters that can be stuck directly to all the materials mentioned.

Decide how the banners will be hung before the guests start working on them. Depending on the size of the banners and the room in which they will be displayed, different methods will work. Some can be hung by attaching string to the banner's top and dangling the banner from a nail. To hang the banner more freely, use a board or broom handle at the top of the banner. Wrap the material around the board or handle and staple it to itself. Then attach wire or cord to each end of the handle and hang it from the ceiling.

It's important that you make hanging decisions before work begins, because in some cases, this will limit working space. For example, if you're going to wrap the top of the banner around a broom handle, people need to work down about six inches from the top of their banner. Otherwise words or symbols will be lost.

PLAN FOR THE EVENING

The Banners' Purpose

The pastor should share the purpose behind the banners. This is not just busy work for happy partygoers. Hopefully the banners will help focus people's attention on Christ and play a part in their determining to be more dedicated to him. His is an informational and pep talk.

Working Units

Divide the group into working units —one unit for each banner. Try to put one leader-type in each group, although that person won't be a designated leader. Leadership should fall naturally as the plans for each unit's banner progress.

Go over the process each unit should follow. They should begin by making sure everyone knows everyone else. They should then brainstorm ideas for their banner. This means they will be suggesting words, shapes, decorations that will go into developing the best possible banner. Remind everyone to keep a brainstorming mindset in the first part of this discussion. This means that everyone should throw in every idea he can think of—even if it doesn't sound so great at first. Perhaps someone else will take it and refine it into the best idea ever.

When all ideas are presented, the unit should pick the best idea and begin planning how the banner will look. It's usually best to sketch a rough of the proposed idea.

The unit should then assign work tasks. Someone could be in charge of cutting the letters. Another person could fringe the material. A third could work to make the symbolic picture.

Encourage the unit to talk as they work. This is, after all, a party. The job has to get done, but if people don't have a good time doing it, half the party's purpose is lost.

Here are some sample banners. The first is an all symbolic banner which would be perfect for either Christmas or Easter. It was developed by Rich Nickel.[1] Choose colors which would add to people's understanding of the symbolism. For example, both circles could be yellow.

The line could be black, and the half circle which represents earth could be green—or perhaps black. The background could be tan.

Of course, these aren't the only workable colors, but plan your poster as a total unit—colors, symbols, words should all blend.

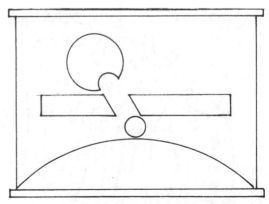

[1]First printed in "Truth and Countertruth" teacher's guide from *Christian Growth* Electives, © 1978 David C. Cook Publishing Co. Used by permission.

This banner symbolically illustrates what we celebrate at Christmas and Easter. God sent his Son to earth, breaking the barrier between man and himself.

Most likely the wording on other banners and the very season in which it is hung would make the symbolism of this wordless banner very clear.

The next banner incorporates words with simple art. Encourage your people to keep all illustrations extremely simple; then they will be easier to execute on the banner background, and more easily understood by people who see them at a distance. This poster might be perfect for Easter. Hands could be black and white felt, and the lettering could be any bright color that will shine out from the background color. Perhaps yellow words on a red background would be good.

It is also possible to plan a whole banner using words only. Usually people would want to hand letter an all-word banner so they can mold the words into a pleasing pattern.

A Thanksgiving banner might look something like this, built around Psalm 30:12.

Color on an all-word banner could be used to emphasize the most important words. The unit might choose *you* and *forever*. Or since it's Thanksgiving, it might pick *Thanks forever* as the focus.

After the Banners
Each unit has probably already seen what the others are doing. But encourage a formal showing. Each group might tell why it chose the direction it did and what some of its other close-running options were.

The laborers are worthy of some good food. Since your house is probably covered with pins and paste and material scraps, don't be too fancy about the food. Why not plan something that can be taken out of the refrigerator and served —no on-the-spot cooking. And don't forget the paper plates.

SANDY'S NO-CRUST PIE

In the blender, combine:
4 eggs
1/2 cup flour
2 cups milk
4 teaspoons soft butter
1/2 cup sugar
1 teaspoon vanilla.
Stir in by hand 1 cup of coconut. Pour into a greased and floured pie pan. Bake for 40 minutes at 350° or until an inserted knife comes out clean.

GERMAN SWEET CHOCOLATE CAKE
---

1 package German chocolate
1/2 cup boiling water
1 cup butter
2 cups sugar
4 egg yolks, unbeaten
1 teaspoon vanilla
1/2 teaspoon salt
1 teaspoon soda
2 1/2 cups sifted cake flour
1 cup buttermilk
4 egg whites
Melt chocolate in boiling water. Cool. Cream butter and sugar until light and fluffy. Add egg yolks one at a time, beating after each. Add chocolate and vanilla. Sift together salt, soda, and flour. Add alternately with buttermilk to chocolate mixture, beating well after each addition. Beat until smooth. Beat egg whites until stiff peaks form. Fold into batter.

Bake at 350° for 30 to 40 minutes.

Coconut Pecan Frosting
1 cup evaporated milk
1 cup sugar
1/4 pound butter
3 egg yolks
1 teaspoon vanilla
Combine in a saucepan and cook over medium heat until mixture thickens (about 12 minutes). Add about 1 1/3 cups coconut and 1 cup chopped pecans. Beat until frosting is cool and thick enough to spread.

RICE PUDDING
---

1 cup water
1/2 cup rice
Cook for seven minutes. Add 1 quart milk and 1/2 stick of butter. Cover and cook 1 1/4 hours on low heat.

Beat 2 eggs. Add to them 1/2 cup sugar and 1/2 cup raisins and 1/2 teaspoon vanilla.

Mix together. Sprinkle with cinnamon and sugar. Serve hot or cold.

SIGHT AND SOUND— SCRIPTURE ALIVE!

Goal: Christians will gain a new appreciation for God's Word as they plan and present a scriptural choral reading.

Christians will work together as a vocal choir—communicating both God's Word and their own sense of unity.

Basic idea: Representatives from different age levels in the church will plan and carry out an illustrated Scripture reading for the morning worship service.

THE PASTOR

He's the key. If he doesn't think a scriptural choral reading is a good idea, don't plan this project party. If he is in favor, ask him to be at the planning event and share, with those who will participate, what the theme of his morning service will be and which Scriptures he has chosen to use. This choral reading is illustrated with slides. As the slides will take several weeks to develop, he will have to have this information three weeks before the presentation Sunday.

WHY CHORAL READING?

How long has it been since you've been excited by Scripture reading? The Children of Israel used to listen for hours to God's Word being read aloud to them. I can't believe that the reader was unexcited about sharing the stories of Abraham and the trials of the prophets and the beautiful language of the psalmist.

But today, am I unfair in saying that most adults read children's fairy tales

with more enthusiasm and expression than they do God's Word? God gave us our voices with which to praise him. Choral reading will help people who never stood before the congregation and praised God to get involved. In this scriptural choral reading, people will be challenged to make the most of God's gift of voice.

I remember the times I've heard Karen read the Bible. I've been amazed! She makes it come alive. She took me along with the Apostle Paul as he spoke to his churches. She made me feel the terror of the disciples on a wind-wild sea. She helped me feel some of the love that went into God's gift of Jesus Christ. Now, I come from a background of well over three decades of Sunday Bible readings. I have heard God's Word stumbled over, droned through, and even shouted. But Karen's reading was something different. She paused where pauses made sense. She let her voice race excitedly through the material that was so special it left the listener breathless. She stopped dead when she came to the mention of sin and its awful consequences. She read with expression about the Christian's responsibility, and I was excited about hearing God's Word read.

Today's project party is designed to put renewed enthusiasm and understanding into the Bible reading at your church.

Choral reading involves talking, using the same vocal grouping and getting much the same effect as a singing choir. I think I enjoy it so much because I come from a Mennonite background where it seemed everyone could sing —without a piano and in perfect four-part harmony. I don't have an awful singing voice, but the closest I've ever come to using it to present special music to the Lord was at a Sunday evening youth group meeting where my brother and I whistled a duet. But speaking! I can talk, and talk with expression. Choral readings allow me to praise God in a special way and I love it. I think there are many people who don't belong in church choirs who would feel the same way I do about choral reading.

The first church in which I heard choral reading used as part of the morning worship was Circle Church in Chicago. At the time, the church had a high student population. One Sunday when the worship centered around the greatness of God, people from lands around the world participated in an unusual choral reading. It began with each person reading the Scripture in his native tongue and concluded with everyone reading the verses together in English, each in his own special accent. What a beautiful around-the-globe reading it was.

WHO TO INVITE

Why not pick an equal number of people from each Sunday school class, starting with the junior class (fifth and sixth graders) and moving up through the adult classes? For example, if you planned for ten people in the choral reading, two would come from the junior class, two from junior high, two from senior high, two from college or young marrieds class, and two from the adult class. You might want to do all the inviting by phone or in person. This is a work session, and in order for it to be successful you have to have five or more attend.

BEFORE THE PARTY

You've got what appears to be a big job, but stick with me. It's really quite simple. You, with perhaps the help of the pastor and your choir director, should develop the basic scriptural choral reading. This will allow you to have copies duplicated before project party time. Each person participating should have his own script.

Remember, this is a scriptural choral reading. You will not be writing a single original word. Every word will come directly from Scripture. A word or phrase may be repeated, but it's against the rules to change words.

Follow these simple steps:

1. Read the passage several times. Really get to know it. Ask yourself which words are most important. Which phrases jump out at you and emphasize what the pastor will be saying the Sunday this reading is read? In order to get to know the passage better, you could do an inductive study of it. For directions on simple inductive Bible study, see pages 66 to 70.

2. Begin to write the script, using the words of the passage. Repeat the sections that you wish to emphasize. Never take away or add words. As you write you should leave a two-inch margin on the left-hand side of the paper, and double space. This will allow those participating to write in the names of the people who will be saying each line and to underline or circle words they feel should be given special expression.

Here's a starter sample from John 3:16, 17.

107

For God loved the world so much
For God loved the world so much
For God loved the world so much that
   he gave his only Son so that anyone
   who believes in him shall not perish
But have eternal life.
For God loved the world so much
God did not send his Son into the
   world to condemn it, but to save it.
Condemn
Save
Condemn
Save
Save, save, save.
For God loved the world so much
   that he gave.

Of course, your passage may be longer than two verses. What I've provided here is just a sample. Look at what I've done. I've started with phrases.

Then I built a comparison between two very different words—condemn and save. The participants will have to decide how best to communicate the difference between the two. Perhaps a strong male voice will throw out the word, "Condemn." The group will respond with a loud, joyful, "Save." The fact that God loved is emphasized in the repetition of the phrase. This phrase could be said matter-of-factly the first time and could build in expression and excitement as people catch the implications—the God of the universe loves everyone; the God of the universe loves me!

WHEN GUESTS ARRIVE
Explain the plan of the evening. The pastor may share what text will be made into a choral reading and how he plans

to use that text in his sermon. You give a little background on the value of choral reading. Explain that guests will be preparing the reading and then talking about slides which would illustrate the reading.

Slides may actually be taken at the party or scheduled for some later time. The final part of the work session will be spent practicing the reading.

Remember that this party must take place at least three weeks before its results are shared with the congregation. You'll need that time to practice the reading several times, take the pictures, get them developed, and coordinate the speaking with the illustrative slides.

INTO THE READING
Pick two people to read the Scripture directly as it is written in the Bible. This will give everyone a feeling for the whole text.

Then divide into two task forces.

Each force is to consider the meaning of the text and how the voices in its group can best portray that meaning. Remind them that every singing combination is a possible speaking combination—whole group together, solo, duet, trio. Give the groups time to experiment, to have fun planning the best way to share Christ.

When parts have been assigned, each group should begin practicing and refining what it has done. Refining would include picking the correct expression, deciding on volume levels, picking special words to emphasize.

Set a time limit on this planning. Go from group to group in the early planning stages to answer any questions, and to make certain the group is headed in the right direction. When there are about five minutes left, give groups a warning so they can put on the final touches.

After the planning of the groups is finished, have each group present what they have done for each other.

From the best in both groups, develop the final script. Use everyone in the reading. Those who don't have special parts will be important to the total choir.

A final script might look something like this:

Alice For God loved the world so much *(softly)*

Alice & Jane For God loved the world so much *(louder)*

All { For God loved the world so much that he gave his only Son so that anyone who believes in him shall not perish *build to a trumpet finish*

Bob But have eternal life. *(joyfully)*

Alice For God loved the world so much. *(softly)*

All { God did not send his son into the world to condemn it, but to save it. *Start softly and slowly. Build to a finish.*

Jack Condemn *(angry, loud)*

Alice Save *(soft)*

Jack Condemn *(loud, anger)*

Alice Save *(louder)*

All Save, save, save. *(very loud, joyful)*

Jack & Alice For *God* loved the *world* so much that he *gave. Emphasize key words.*

SOME HINTS FOR BETTER CHORAL READINGS

A choral group should pick a speaking leader, someone with an expressive voice. Others will copy his expression in all of the group reading parts. This will keep the group from sounding like the waves that wash in an endless rhythm upon the sand. That predictable pattern can be boring. At best, an expressionless choir communicates only words, not the meaning of those words. A leader is also responsible for starting each total group part. This eliminates the awful false starts when everyone knows it's time to talk, but no one is willing to start first.

The most difficult parts of the choral reading will be those sections in which everyone speaks together.

Overlap: After your group has gotten the hang of choral reading, you might want to try some more creative things. For example, it is interesting to have someone begin speaking before the last person is quite done speaking—especially if he is repeating the same phrase.

Diagrammed, the reading would look like this:

Person 1:
For God loved the world so much
Person 2:   For God loved the world so much

The words "the world" and "For God" overlap. This takes a lot of practice because you'll have a natural tendency to wait until the other person has stopped speaking before you start. If you do use this technique, you might want to use it several times so people in the congregation realize that the group planned this; they didn't just make a mistake.

Positioning: Have the voice chorale stand in groupings that help present the message. In this choral reading, you will be illustrating with slides. So the group might stand in the back of the church.

In readings without slides, it might be appropriate to have the groups divide into two and speak back and forth to each other across the church.

In one missions choral reading, the leader stood in the center of the congregation, and the rest of the group divided into four and stood in the four corners of the church—representing the four corners of the world. The leader gave the message of salvation, and the groups responded with Scripture verses that shared their questions and responses.

Expressive faces: If the choral group stands where the rest of the congregation can see it, people's faces must show the type of expression their voices are using. John 3:16 is filled with excitement and drama. The faces of those who accept the "saved" message must show their feelings or the message is dimmed. The people who play the "condemned" lines should use their vocal and facial expressions to communicate the awfulness of that decision.

Eye contact: When the readers can be seen by the congregation, they should establish eye contact with them. The speakers have practiced their parts. They will know many of their lines by heart from the repetition. At many points in the reading, they can look up from their papers and at the congregation. Eye contact says, "We're doing this because we care about you. Please listen." And in response, the congregation may do just that.

Many people fear that if they look up for the parts they know, they will lose their place on the sheets when they need to read again. I use the thumb of my left hand as a line mark. I move it down the page as the reading progresses. I can look up at any time and get my place again in a second just by checking the line above my thumb.

THE SLIDES

Take a break in your choral reading practice to discuss what slides might best illustrate the passage. Should the pictures be literal, or should they convey a mood or an idea?

List everyone's ideas. Then as a group pick those that are best.

Either take the pictures now, or assign someone to be in charge of taking them. If you have a senior high or college student who enjoys photography, this would be an excellent way to use his talents for Christ.

Here are a few ideas that might work on John 3:16 (*The Living Bible*):

For God loved the world so much	Missionary pictures, flashed at 5 second intervals.
For God loved the world so much	Pictures of people from our congregation. Pictures flashed quickly. Many of these are probably available from people who have attended the church for a while.
For God loved the world so much that he gave his only Son so that anyone who believes in him shall not perish	Several sunrise pictures, or plant pictures to symbolize new beginnings. Hands of a child in different positions might do the same thing.
But have eternal life	Picture of smiling children.
For God loved the world so much	More church pictures.
God did not send his son into the world to condemn it, but to save it.	Picture or symbol of Christ—perhaps a statue in the church or a painting in the Sunday school room.
Condemn	Match lighted.
Save	Match blown out—smoke still rising.
Condemn	Match lighted.
Save	Match blown out—smoke still rising.
Save, save, save	Bright colors—yellow, red, green. These could be materials with lights behind them.
For God loved the world so much that he gave.	Several quick pictures of people clapping —maybe just their hands.

Take more pictures than you'll need. Shoot from different angles and change the settings for each shot. This will give you an opportunity for choice, and raise your chances of having a very professional final project.

PRAYER TIME

People have been involved in Bible study in this party. First, they have simply read the Bible. Then they studied it to see how they could best communicate it to others. Some may have memorized short portions as they practiced. Finally, they visually interpreted what they had learned. The slides became a picture paraphrase.

Prayer naturally follows this study.

Guide the prayer by suggesting topics. Ask people to limit themselves to sentence prayers on the topic. They may pray as often as they wish.

Allow people to stay on one topic as long as they are continuing to contribute. When you feel everyone has finished with that topic, suggest the next.

I like this type of guided sentence prayers. When I was a child learning to pray in public, it took me most of the prayer meeting to gather up courage. I would mentally list the things I might talk about and go over them in my mind. By the time I prayed my recited sentences, I had lost most of my enthusiasm. But in prayer like this, the topic is chosen for me. People who pray easily in public won't pray around Robin's barn, leaving me nothing to share aloud with God and his people. And since

it's fine just to pray a single sentence, those who are newcomers to shared prayers may dare to try.

Topics of prayer will vary, of course, with your situation. If I were giving this party right now, I might use a list like this:

Thank God for what his Word means to me—perhaps singling out a special verse.

Praise to God for our church leaders who regularly share God's Word with me.

Request for excellence in the choral reading project so his name will be glorified; people might mention their individual fears about participating in the choral reading.

Prayer for people who will be hearing the reading. Perhaps some might mention those who need salvation.

Host or hostess should close, thanking God for the food.

FOOD

Speaking can make people very hungry! Why not provide the makings for great sandwiches, and let people put their own original creations together? Then each person should cut his sandwich in half and exchange a half with someone else. He might give the half to someone he has enjoyed getting to know better.

Or, you could get several long loaves of French bread, fill them with sandwich goodies, and slice off a sandwich for everyone. You might include luncheon meats, cheese, shredded lettuce, tomatoes, egg salad, tuna salad, or the following sandwich spreads.

MINCED CORNED BEEF

Minced corned beef combined with pickle relish and moistened with mayonnaise between slices of cracked whole wheat bread is great. Add lettuce leaf for freshness.

CREAM CHEESE SPREAD

Blend two packages of cream cheese, two Tablespoons of cream, 1/2 small (grated) cucumber, and 1 Tablespoon grated onion. When blended smooth, spread on whole wheat bread.

For novelty, add cake coloring to make the spread bright green.

KIDS' SPECIAL

Try peanut butter with sliced banana on top. Or peanut butter and grape jelly, a junior all-time favorite.

HAM BROILER

Mix 1 cup ground boiled ham, 1 cup grated cheese, 1/2 cup condensed tomato soup, 1/2 teaspoon mustard, and 1/2 teaspoon horse radish. Toast bread and spread with this mixture. Toast again under broiler.

DRIED BEEF

Try dried beef between dark bread that has been spread with butter and cream cheese.

WALNUT-CHEESE SPECIAL

Soften one package of sharp-flavored cheese spread. Add two Tablespoons catsup, pinch of salt. Add onion juice to taste. Add 1/2 cup chopped walnut meats, and spread on rye bread.

CORN BREAD SANDWICH

Make corn bread. Let it cool. Put 1 cup milk in double boiler with 1 pound of cheese cut into small squares. Leave until melted and blended. Slice corn bread and cover with a slice of fried ham. Top with second slice of corn bread. Pour melted cheese sauce over sandwich. Top with a slice of crisp bacon and serve hot.

WAYS TO EXPAND THE CHORAL READING IDEA

We have presented plans for a complete "Sight and Sound" project party. But when people respond to the type of creativity this party demands, it may mean they have the talents and gifts to do other things in the church.

Paraphrases

Young people often enjoy making their own paraphrases of Scripture—setting the biblical situations into their own twentieth century world.

An example of a paraphrase of the twenty-third Psalm will help you see what I mean. You might also read this example to young people just to give them an idea of what to try. This is how one person thinks David might have written the twenty-third Psalm if David had lived on the West side of Chicago in the 1980s.

The Lord walks guard beside me; I won't panic.
He keeps me cool like I was under a street light.
He leads me down safe alleys.
He turns up the heat and puts glass in the
*   window.*
He don't let me do nothing to shame him.
The Sharks got knives. My friends got needles,
*   but I'm clean.*
I got Jesus with me. He never cuts out.
My enemies see me full without busting no
*   heads or rolling no dice or stealing no*
*   wheels, and I tell them Jesus done it.*
I got joy.
The joy will just keep on coming for the rest
*   of my days, and I got me a place with*
*   Jesus forever.*

This may not be the way you would
write this psalm in your neighborhood,
but is there any doubt that the person
who did write it knows what David felt
and feels the security of God's protection
and love?

Once the paraphrase is done, it can
easily be developed into a choral reading.

Scripture Collages
Sometimes the message we want to share
is found in various passages all through
the Bible. Encourage people to research
the best verses to get across their message
and develop a choral reading collage.
What a great way to learn what's in the
Bible. Can't you just hear a senior high
kid saying, "There's this great verse
about having a thankful attitude somewhere in this Book, and I'm going to keep
looking until I find it."

Scripture Songs
Real singing here! A lot of talented young
writers are setting Scripture to music. It's
an excellent way to learn Bible verses.

If you have talented musicians in your
church, you might want to share several
of these Bible verse song records with
them and encourage them to try writing
their own. Artistic friends could illustrate
the song with slides.

Sight and Sound and Sound
In addition to the choral reading and the
slides, try a musical background. What a
great multimedia way to praise God.
Careful—this will take a lot of work.
Make certain the final product reflects
the message of God's Word and that all
people involved realize that the purpose
of the reading is to glorify God, not
to glorify the people who participate.

In all areas, as we work to serve God,
we should strive for excellence. Not many
people would say aloud, "God will accept
a lot less than total excellence from
us, so why work so hard?" Yet often that
seems to be the attitude toward much
we offer to him in the name of praise and
worship. Aim high. Aim at excellence.
Let your choral readings—and other
responses to God—speak loudly to the
fact that our God deserves nothing less.

PROJECT: MISSION AWARENESS
A Party to Plan an All-Church Party

Goal: Church members who are
interested in missions will meet to plan
an all-church mission awareness party.

Basic idea: This is a project to plan a
party—a party within a party. People will
meet and plan a complete mission

114

awareness evening for the church, perhaps scheduling a Sunday evening for the event. At the planning session, people will learn methods of structuring a good party, and they will have the positive experience of sharing their ideas and seeing them become part of an all-church event.

I've been part of three mission awareness parties, and I'm in the middle of planning a fourth. They can be great fun; they can also be great learning experiences.

At the first party, I was one of three adult guests. The whole evening had been planned by a group of sixth grade Pioneer Girls. That evening they shared a little of what they had learned about God's work in one other country. Included in the evening were tapes from that country's missionaries, a few cultural games, a report on the country from encyclopedia sources, and a meal that was typical in that country. I left absolutely certain that there wasn't a girl in that room who wouldn't remember to pray for the missionaries and Christians in their chosen country.

At the second party, Dee and I worked together to plan an evening of cross-cultural experiences for people who were part of our church's missions task force, the Global Community Module. At the time I had just returned from three years as a missionary teacher in Japan and she was thinking about becoming a missionary in Japan. About forty people participated in the games and Japanese meal. A great learning experience, and yes, Dee is now on the mission field full time.

While Jack and I were dating we

planned a third missions party. Gladys, our good friend, had just returned from Russia where she had traveled for several weeks with Russian-speaking Christians. What stories she had to tell. Jack and I invited about thirty people to a Russian supper followed by Gladys' slides and stories. Jack and I learned how much we enjoyed exercising hospitality and our friends got a unique glimpse into missions. Our fourth party is coming up and it will be patterned after the Russian one. Only this time Gladys has just returned from Red China. She'll have new stories and new pictures, and best yet, we will gain a greater understanding of our prayer responsibility for this newly opened land.

All the missions parties worked! People are interested in missions; parties allow them to freshen that interest by coming at the subject in a unique way.

WHO TO INVITE
First, clear the whole idea with the pastor, and decide with him when the party should be held. Include him in the planning for the party. Beforehand, invite ten to fifteen people who are already interested in missions and sharing their interest with others in the church. Since this is a work party, you may want to invite everyone in person.

Let them know that this will also be a fun evening, but it is basically a party to plan a party. Encourage them to come with ideas for a missions party that would benefit the whole church family.

THE EVENING'S AGENDA
Here's one way to structure your evening. I'll be following it as I give ideas that

might spark others in your group.
1. Pick a featured country.
2. Set goals for the all-church mission party.
3. Brainstorm ideas for the all-church mission party.
4. Brainstorm food ideas.
5. Assign all task and prayer groups.

Pick a featured country.
Any one will do. You might want to encourage people to pick one on which you have some information. For example, I've been to Venezuela, Mexico, Japan. Those would be logical countries for me to suggest. I also know missionaries in France and Greece and could get information from those countries.

It makes sense to pick a country in which the church is supporting a missionary.

When all countries are suggested, take a vote to decide which country will be the focal point of the Mission Awareness evening for the whole church.

Set goals for the all-church mission party.
Without goals, you really don't know what you want to accomplish, and you certainly won't be able to evaluate what you accomplished when the party is over. Setting these goals as a group will help people feel the importance of what they will be doing.

Everyone should brainstorm the goals, and the group should pick those they wish to see met. These should be written, and each person at this planning session should receive a copy. He should keep these goals in mind as he plans and prays for the coming event.

Here are sample goals:
That our church will gain a greater understanding of the mission work in (the country).
That (missionary) will get prayer and financial support.
That our church young people will get a greater burden for missions.

Brainstorm ideas for the all-church mission party.
Now it's time to talk about what will happen on the evening of the all-church party. Encourage everyone to throw out his ideas. Ask planners to think "participation." Many people have never really participated in a missions evening. They have come and sat and listened. How could that pattern be livened up a bit by getting everyone actively involved?

I've included some of the ideas I've had. You might want to share one or two of the better ones with the group just to get the juices flowing.

Write to the missionary we know in our chosen country and ask him to send us a five-minute tape talking about what he does on a typical day. Ask him to include one or two specific prayer requests.
Plan a playlet on life in the chosen country. Perhaps some people in the congregation have visited the country and could help. This might also be an area in which the older elementary children could get involved.
Show slides of the country. (If you picked a missionary who is on furlough you can have him show his work. Many missions have slides available with printed or taped scripts for churches to use. A few have representatives

116

around the country who visit and speak upon request.

Plan a project offering. Make copies of a map of this country and give each person a copy. Explain the project and ask people to write on the map the amount of money they are able to give toward the project. (You might ask people to sign their pledges and write in the date by which they will give the promised amount.) Anyone, even those unable to give, who also wants to play a most important part should write the word *prayer* on the map. All should be placed in the offering. It would be excellent if the pledges could be counted during the evening so people will know immediately if their project will be completed.

Be creative in your choice of projects. For example, I know one church that earned enough money to send builders to Mexico to build irrigation ditches with the Mexican Christians. Mexicans were so pleased with their willing partners that the group accomplished twice as much as its stated goal. Non-Christians shared with their neighbors that these Christians really seemed to live what they talked.

Another church raised money to send a high school teen to the mission field for several weeks to get a firsthand feel for what God was doing in other cultures.

Plan games. Does the country have any special ones that could be played in the available space? Check an encyclopedia, and resource people. Or you could use things from these countries to spark original games that would give the flavor of that land.

For example, you could have a chopstick relay if your country were Hong Kong. People in Hong Kong probably don't have chopstick relays, but this game will give your church people an understanding of how difficult it is to learn to eat in different ways. They will gain an appreciation of the missionary that they may not have had before. In a chopstick relay, the group would be divided into teams, and a bowl of grapes would be placed at the far end of the room from each line. At the starting bell, the first person in each line would take the chopsticks, run to the bowl, pick up a grape with the chopsticks, eat it, dash back to his line, and give the chopsticks to the second person, who would repeat the procedure. The first line finished wins.

Or if your country is Colombia, divide into teams for a rhythm band contest. Teams have ten minutes to collect their instruments (combs, wastepaper cans, etc.) and practice a song using a South American beat.

Plan a postcard blitz. Supply postcards to people at the all-church party and ask them to write immediately to the missionaries they know in that country. One person would be in charge of sending the postcards two or three at a time over the next month or so.

A variation of this would be to start a round robin letter with each person at the all-church party adding a few paragraphs. Or easier, talking a few minutes on a tape.

Plan several roleplay situations in which people at the planning meeting would demonstrate some of the missionary's typical experiences.

Talk about decorations. How could the room reflect the country? Perhaps a curio display, travel posters, or a mural done by the high school department could be considered.

Consider news reports from this country. Cover the secular as well as the Christian events. This might even be done as a newscast with an anchorman saying, "And now we take you to the country of _____ for an update." Other reporters could read their items. Again, this is an excellent project for the junior high and senior high young people.

Now obviously, you'll be developing ideas that are best suited to your situation. Use my list to get a start, but never forget that you are planning an evening that is unique to your situation.

Brainstorm food ideas.
You might want to plan an entire meal that will be much like the meals served in this country.

Or you might want to plan a rice meal, to give the church people an idea of the poverty meals eaten by many people in third and fourth world nations.

Or you could supply snacks from around the world. Each snack should be labeled by name and country. Many of these are now available in the specialty food sections of many grocery stores.

Here are the recipes from my second mission awareness party. If you choose an oriental country, you might want to copy it. Otherwise, it can serve as a sample of the type of thing that is possible.

This meal will cost about $3.00 per person. You might want to encourage those who are able to help defray the costs.

SALAD

Serves 24
6 heads lettuce
12 small green onions with stems, chopped fine
3 large cans mandarin oranges
healthy sprinkling of parsley flakes
Dressing:
1/4 cup wine vinegar
1/4 cup lemon juice
1 cup sugar
healthy dash of pepper
6 cups salad oil
Shake well and pour over salad just before serving. Top with carameled almonds.
Carameled Almonds:
2 cups slivered, blanched almonds
1 cup sugar
Combine in skillet over very low heat. Push almonds around until the sugar melts and covers them. Let cool; break apart.

FLANK STEAK TERIYAKI
---

6 pounds flank steak cut into 1-inch strips. Have butcher cut with the grain of the meat. Roll into pinwheels. Fasten with toothpicks, and set aside in a shallow pan.
Marinade:
3 teaspoons ground ginger
3 Tablespoons cooking oil
1/4 cup cooking sherry
1 1/2 cup soy sauce
3/4 cup sugar
2 cloves garlic, mashed
Mix together marinade ingredients and pour over meat. Cover and let stand in refrigerator for three days. If marinade doesn't completely cover the pinwheels. turn them over after about a day and a half.

118

Shortly before serving time, place flank steak pinwheels on broiler. Brush with marinade once and broil 5 to 7 inches from the heat for another 7 minutes. Turn; brush again with marinade and broil about 7 minutes longer, or until done.

Serve teriyaki with pineapple rings and rice.

If you want to add a vegetable dish, mix canned bean sprouts with French style green beans.

DESSERT

Sherbet is appropriate. You might want to add a few rice crackers, now available in many foreign food sections of the grocery store as well as at specialty stores such as Pier 1. These crackers have various names, but *O Sembi* is usually written on the packet somewhere.

Or if you really want to have an unusual dessert, try Kaki Pudding (persimmon).
Serves 24
6 cups persimmon pulp
3 cups milk
6 cups sugar
6 cups flour
1/2 teaspoon salt
6 Tablespoons butter
1/4 cup soda
1 1/2 teaspoons vanilla
4 cups nuts
Mix ingredients together. Bake in a greased 8-inch pan for 1 hour in a 300-350° oven.

A WORD ABOUT
PLANNING MEETING SNACKS:
You might want to try some finger foods from different countries, perhaps purchasing everything from the foreign food section of the food store. Lots of things are available. Throughout the evening you could announce what you are serving and pass things around as people are working. Here are some things I know my store carries:

marshmallow chocolates from Israel
O Sembi rice crackers
dry roasted peanuts
guacamole dip and taco chips
mandarin oranges (serve with toothpicks)
fortune cookies
rice puffs

Assign all task and prayer groups.
Now it's time to assign task groups. What you have decided to do in the missions party will determine what groups you need. Here are some possible groups:

1. Prayer groups—meeting weekly until the party
2. Advertisement group—perhaps contacting each person from the church personally
3. Food committee—this doesn't mean that they will do all the food work. But they will decide what needs to be done and head up the process.
4. Mission awareness program committee

A MISSIONS SIMULATION
After the task group has completed its work, you may want to play a missions simulation to give them the feeling of what happens to a missionary when he goes to a new and unfamiliar culture. It's

a fun and silly game, but it's designed to help participants empathize with those God calls to serve him in this unique, difficult way. One thing is for sure! If your people take this simulation game seriously, the new missionaries from your church will be upheld in prayer like never before.

In simulation games, there is no winner or loser. It's an experience game rather than a competition game like checkers. In a simulation, people are involved in a simulated or pretend reality. A new cultural experience is reduced in size so that people can participate in it for a few minutes and gain a bit of an under-standing of what culture shock is. In this mission simulation, you won't make people feel all the frustration of learning a new language and new customs, but you can let them feel for a few minutes some of the frustrations of being different, of not belonging and fitting in, of being lonely and ineffective.

Careful! Simulations can change people's attitudes. This simulation could turn people on to missions in a new way because for a half hour or so, they were there!

I've chosen to develop a simulation about cultural differences because this is an area in which I have faced frustration. And I think others who have lived in different cultures would agree.

I remember being in Venezuela as a short-term missionary. I thought it would be dandy if I organized the little boys at the vacation Bible school into baseball teams. We used our arms as bats and hard lemons as balls. It was great fun until the mission leader explained that baseball was a no-no! In Venezuela

people bet on baseball games in the same way Americans do on the horses. So as a testimony to nonbelievers, Christians don't play baseball.

The same thing happens, of course, to people who come into our Western culture.

One missionary kid who had spent all his teen years in Japan came back to the States for college. He was thrown out of a shoe store the first week back when he told the manager that he wore size twenty-eight. The manager thought he was just another smarting off, rude kid. The boy had a terrible time getting up enough nerve to go to another store.

CULTURE SHOCK
A Missionary Simulation Experience

Explanation
When missionaries go into a new culture, they try to conform to the habits and customs of the people, as long as they don't violate the principles taught in the Bible.

That can be terribly hard, because we are so used to our old cultural habits. Add the pressures of learning a new language, new living and eating situations, and removal from former close friends and familiar places. It's only through God's help that missionaries survive the first year.

Today we're going to go through a culture shock as we pretend to be missionaries entering the unusual country of Flockland.

In this simulation, our language will remain English, of course, but we will make the experience difficult by setting up a crazy series of cultural imperatives.

Project: Mission Awareness

These are things newcomers must do if they expect to communicate effectively with the people in Flockland.

The list is silly, of course, but then who's to say that the cultural rules are any stranger than our own—we're just more used to our own.

Cultural Rules

(Here you can make your own list or use mine. Or combine yours and mine. You might want to place these on a chalkboard or large sheet of paper so they remain in front of everyone during this first part of the simulation.)

In Flockland, a cultured person never uses pronouns—only complete names.

In Flockland, when people meet, they jump up and down twice and clap once. When they part, they rub noses.

In conversation, it is considered very poor manners to laugh or show your teeth. Pleasure is shown by rubbing the tongue quickly back and forth across the lower lip.

Conversations in Flockland are limited to two minutes. Longer conversations indicate the person is lazy, making poor use of time and vocabulary.

No one sits with his legs touching.

Everyone snaps his fingers in a regular rhythm when he is talking with someone of the opposite sex, even a spouse, if he's in public.

A refined person never covers more than ten inches with each step.

A sign of friendship is to pull a hair from your head and present it to the person to whom you're talking. This can also be a sign that you're telling the truth.

Upon leaving a person, you should bestow a wish upon him. For example, "I wish you rain for your potatoes."

When a Flockland person sits, it is improper for him to lean back. Usually he perches on the edge of the chair.

Spend five minutes getting used to the rules. Interact as people of Flockland. At the end of this time, the list of cultural rules will be taken down and you will be asked to act on them without seeing them.

Note mistakes others make and correct them. This is not the main part of the simulation; it's more a practice for it.

It will be impossible for most people to get through the five minutes without making many errors in the etiquette of Flockland. Of course, the rules are ridiculous, but in many lands—Japan, Zaire, France, etc.—if a missionary disobeys cultural rules his credibility is lessened, the people who will listen to his message are fewer, and in some primitive cultures, his very life may be in danger.

At the end of the five minutes, allow time for people to share some of their feelings and their experiences. If necessary, get conversation going with a few questions:

How did you feel after the five minutes? Silly? Tired? A failure?

To us these things are silly. But consider a foreign student coming to our country. What things in our culture might he consider funny, strange?

The Simulation

Divide the participants into two equal groups. One group will be the native Flockland people. They are 100 percent at ease with themselves and their culture.

In order to illustrate this, they should act normally. We will all assume that they are doing the list of things that are culturally right in Flockland.

The burden lies with the second group. They will be the missionaries, and they must remember all the rules of Flockland. (Take the posted rules down.)

It is the responsibility of the second group of people to try to build friendships with Flockland people while remembering all the cultural rules and trying to obey them.

Whenever the missionary makes a mistake, the national should simply walk away from him. Nationals and missionaries should interact for about five to eight minutes.

Remember, the one group acts perfectly normal and we assume it is obeying all the rules. The other group represents the culturally struggling missionary.

If you have time, you might want to switch groups.

After the end of the simulation, debrief. These questions will help:

How many of you feel you laid a friendship base? Did you concentrate more on making friends or on your cultural correctness?

How realistic do you think it is to assume that nationals will turn off the message of Christ if the missionary violates his cultural rules?

What part does the Holy Spirit play in the communication of Christ in a real cross-cultural experience?

What have you learned from this experience?

This game is primarily developed for a group that is already interested in missions. It is not recommended for the total missions awareness party. However, you may want to choose four people to demonstrate the final part of the game for the whole church and then discuss what they felt and what this taught them about new missionaries and the need for backup people at home to pray.

6

GOD BLESS OUR HOME

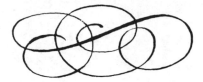

CELEBRATE THE PHYSICAL FAMILY—that wonderfully diverse group of people who live together under one roof! Ideas on bringing the church family together would not be complete without a few directed at the immediate family.

In 1970, the most recent year on record, there were four divorces per 1,000 people and 10.9 marriages. At no other time in history has the world needed more to see positive examples of what Christ can mean in a home.

A HOUSE DEDICATION
This Home, Lord, Is Yours!

Objective: A Christian family will dedicate its home to God in the presence of special friends.

Basic idea: Family members will plan a dedication of their home, inviting their close friends as witnesses and participants. In this dedication they will be saying that this house, the things that are in it, and the people who live in it are God's, and he is in control.

House dedications are usually for people who have just moved into a new home, but that's certainly no absolute. If you like the idea and you've never dedicated your home, why not plan your own celebration? Better seven years late than not at all!

You might also want to share the idea with people in your congregation who have moved—each year more than eighteen people in every 100 change homes.

Jack and I have been part of two house dedications. Gil and Ruth and their two young daughters allowed us and several other friends to help plan their dedication. It was a meaningful experience.

And then, of course, we dedicated our own house several months ago.

House dedications make a lot of sense. At the beginning of marriage, Christians plan a special ceremony asking God to be a third partner in the relationship. That commitment in front of friends makes the whole event more special. The imprint of God's presence in the life of the bride and groom is not easily erased.

In the house dedication, the home is treated with somewhat the same seriousness. It forces the family to be more aware of the presence of God. They have erected a caution against using the house and the people in it incorrectly.

And just as the Christian marriage ceremony is a witness to the world of our determination to be different, so is a Christian home dedication.

I'm going to share our house dedication ideas with you. Use parts from it in your own dedication, but add your own ideas. Make your home dedication truly unique—just as your family is.

GUESTS
We kept our guest list small, limiting it to people we thought would enjoy participating in this type of celebration.

To each single and couple who were invited, we gave an assignment. We wanted our friends to feel a little responsibility for the event—for the success of our witness and our home. We want them to pray for us, and if they think we are headed for trouble, we

INVITATION SAMPLE

We are dedicating our house to God.
Won't you come and be part of our festivities?
Sunday Brunch 2 P.M.

want them to feel close enough to us to tell us.

Our invitations were handwritten, and each included the special assignment.

Individual assignments included:

Please pray a prayer of dedication for our living room. (Or the kitchen, or the bedroom.)

Please bring a verbal gift that you would like us to use in our new home—this should be something you would wish for us.

(To the pastor) We would like you to share what God expects of us in our new home.

These different assignments allowed for a variety of serious and lighter inter-action. Our dedication followed this format (approximately 45 minutes):

1. Welcome to our home (5 minutes).
2. An explanation of a house dedication (2-3 minutes).
3. A walk through the house. Prayers of dedication for the assigned rooms (15 minutes).
4. Verbal gifts in the living room (10 minutes).
5. Brief words from the pastor (5 minutes).
6. (Optional) Prayer of exorcism (1 minute).
7. Vows of the family (3-4 minutes).
8. Brunch.

A CLOSER LOOK
AT OUR DEDICATION
1. Welcome to our home.
This might be the place for a little history of the house, especially if it is not new. Ours is well over sixty years old,

and our neighbors have shared several interesting, if conflicting, stories about the people who have lived there before us. The son of the first owner, or so the story goes, was an illustrator for hot dog commercials!

2. An explanation of a house dedication. Jack and I wrote what we wanted to say:

Jack: Sometimes we feel like misplaced apartment people, but deep down we are beginning to belong to this house. Living here has been a day-by-day educational process.

Marlene: I'm forever noticing noises I can't identify and rushing off to the basement to put my ear to the furnace or water heater to determine just where the shake, rattle, or roar is coming from. It beats me what I intend to do when I find it!

Jack: More than anything, we want our house to be a home where God is glorified. So we've asked you to participate in our giving of our house to the Lord. You are very, very welcome.

3. A walk through the house.
Prayers of dedication for the assigned rooms.

The prayers people offered for our rooms were beautiful.

Living room
God and Father, may this doorway welcome friends and strangers into a room filled with your love and watched by your Spirit. May these walls keep the confidences of heartfelt conversations and reverberate with fellowship and

laughter. May these floors uphold weary feet, bringing comfort to those in need. May these chairs become symbols of the encircling of your love by those who partake of the hospitality of this household.

Kitchen
(At our first exposure to a house dedication, Jack and I were assigned the kitchen. I think Jack's love for cooking and his excitement about what can happen between friends around food led to our being assigned the kitchen. We did our presentation in the form of a choral reading.)

Both: Father, for Gil and Ruth, we dedicate this kitchen to your service.
Jack: We dedicate the food that will be prepared here. Keep the family thankful and aware that many whom you love never have tasted so bountifully of your gifts. Thank you, Lord, for the creative possibilities you have left open to us cooks—all the many foods and colors and tastes—to mix or spice or eat raw. Thank you for the opportunity to exercise this talent daily in love for the family and for those you bring to eat in this home.
Marlene: We dedicate the hours Ruth and Gil and the girls spend in this small area working *together*—planning, cooking, cleaning up. Keep those times free from frustration and complaining. Use this space and the tasks done here to bind the family into a working, loving, sharing unit.
Jack: We dedicate the hours that Ruth and Gil and the girls will spend in this small area *alone*—planning, cooking,

cleaning up. Often the jobs done here allow the workers mind-drifting time. Guide this drifting toward thoughts of you. While the potatoes are being peeled or dishes are being wiped, this room can become a "closet of prayer." Lord, we dedicate these free moments to you.
Both: Father, for Gil and Ruth and their family, we dedicate this kitchen to your service. Amen.

Bedroom
Kris and Tom had just gotten married, and as a rather happy joke, Jack and I asked them to dedicate our bedroom. When they finished their reading, there was hardly a dry eye in the room. And Jack leaned over to me and said, "I'm glad we're married."

Tom: Lord, this is a room of rest.
Kris: And love. Two of the most delightful gifts that come from you.
Tom: Rest, sleep, slumber. "Now I lay me down to sleep. I pray you, Lord my soul to keep."
Kris: Sleep that knits up the raveled sleeve of care.
Both: How incredibly good it feels to ease your aching bones down, stretching your length uncramped. To lie folded in your darling's arms, to kiss, embrace, enjoy.
Tom: And then to sleep, peace attending, all through the night.
Kris: Waking to a bright, new sunlit morning, you see each other's faces. And true, plain hearts do in those faces rest.
Tom: Mellow is the feeling in the morning when you rise.

128

Both: Lord, in this room, two share your
   love; as one they do recline.
Kris: In rest be here.
Tom: In love be here.
Kris: Refresh them in the quiet nights.
Tom: And at those touching times.
Both: Hold them near you from dusk 'til
   dawn. Amen.

4. Verbal gifts in the living room.
After our walk through the rooms and
their dedication, we all returned to the
living room for the presentation of verbal
gifts some of our friends had brought.
   Here's an example from Rita and Bob,
an engaged couple.
   "We wish you a personality blender.
This unique appliance works something
like a food blender. Instead of combining
different food ingredients, the personality blender helps you mix different
people into enriching friendships.
   "Our personality blender does not
work with rotary beaters, nor is it
powered by electricity. Instead,
personality blending is accomplished by
your word of welcome, by your thought-
ful introductions and conversation
starters, by the comfortable and pleasant
surroundings your home provides, by
the fun activities you plan.
   "Your blender gets its power from your
love for Christ and your concern for
other people. Use it with Christ's help to
share your home and your friendship."
   Monette and Bob decided to be totally
humorous with their gift, and they sang
it to the tune of "We Wish You a Merry
Christmas." Here are several verses.

We wish you no faulty furnace
We wish you no leaking rooftops
We wish you no cracking plaster
And no need to call cops.

We wish you lots of green plants
And flowers blooming year 'round
And in your home much music
And from neighbors no sound!

We wish you cash for mortgage
We wish you cash for taxes
We wish you bread for table
With sugar and molasses!

   Not great poetry, you say? Well, you're
wrong. It was one of the loveliest gifts
we ever received.

5. Brief words from the pastor.
How very special it was to hear from our
pastor what our responsibilities before
God are. At the end of his five-minute
talk, he presented Jack and me with a
little hand-made sand and cement castle.
"This will remind you," he said, "that
this shingled 'castle' that you are buying
should be a reflection of your inner
spiritual castle."
   Then he led the group in singing "Joy
is the flag flown from the castle of my
heart when the king is in residence there."

6. (Optional) Prayer of exorcism.
We asked Karen to pray a prayer of
exorcism for our house. Here is her
prayer:

Now, Holy Spirit, come
And fill this house with your presence.
Permeate the atmosphere, the density,
   the concreteness of this place.
Breathe here.

Breathe spiritual breath.
  Begone any choking adversary, any
  evil breath-taker, any life-robbing,
  stealing dark thing.
Let this be a hallowed place,
Consecrated to the Lord, the Life-
  Breather, the Breath-Giver.
Cover this house with the blood of Christ.
  Mark it as sacred,
  Filled with him and none other.
  Begone any who are not under this
    mercy.
  And come Breath.
  Come from the four winds, O Breath.
Breathe upon all who dwell within here,
That they may live.
  Come Breath.

7. Vows of the family
Ruth and Gil included their two young
daughters in this part of their dedication.
The father asked each girl simple
questions which allowed her to share her
beautiful child's faith that Jesus was
indeed part of their family. His questions
to his preschool and young elementary
daughters were:

What room in the house do you like best?
Who are your new playmates? What do
  you do together?
Why do you think Jesus gave us this
  special house?
What would you like to thank Jesus for?
How do you know that Jesus is part of our
  family?

  The children's responses dedicated
that house to God as completely as the
parents'.
  Vows are very special things. Let me
share what Jack and I said, but use it
only as a pattern. When you write your

own, ask yourselves why you are
dedicating the house to God and what
you mean by the phrase—House
Dedication. Everything you speak should
be your intention. These are not just
pretty words. They are promises made
before God for which he will hold you
accountable.

Our Vows
Jack: I vow before God and you, our
  friends, to work hard on our marriage
  —the real structure of this house. I
  will love Marlene and share her excite-
  ments and disappointments. I will
  remember that she is my home, and
  this building is just the shingled
  structure where that home resides.
Marlene: I vow before God, and you, our
  friends, to work hard on our marriage.
  I will respect Jack as my husband and
  my best friend. I will build him up and
  support him. I know that this house
  loses its heart when he's not here.
Jack: Through the home that Marlene
  and I are creating, we vow to remain
  aware and sensitive to our Creator and
  to acknowledge ourselves as servants
  to whom he has given this very special
  assignment—to live, grow, and serve
  on North Spring Street.
Marlene: I want this house to be a place
  where people feel comfortable and
  welcome. I vow to do my part to make
  hospitality a key word in our partner-
  ship with God. I want those who walk
  through the door to know that God is
  here, and that he's as pleased as we
  are that guests have come.
Jack: God, thank you for this house and
  what you are going to do with it and
  with us. Thank you for the laughter

that has already been a part of our two
months here. For the little things,
thanks—for the furnace man and for
discovering how to fix the garbage
disposal.

Marlene: Thank you for the laughter
that will come. Give us the strength
we will need to go through the difficult
times and the times when we fail each
other and you.

Jack: Give us the wisdom to continue
building this home—not with bricks
and shingles but with love and understanding and excitement.

Marlene: Thank you for your creation
of our first home.

Jack: We dedicate ourselves and this
home to you.

You may want to end your vows with
a song in which the words and music say
exactly what you want them to say. If you
can't find one, then pick a song that
everyone knows and write words that
allow you to praise God for the house he
gave.

This example of original words to a
familiar melody is built around "Come Ye
Thankful People, Come."

God, your thankful people come
Raising songs of this new home.
For the roof and for the floor
Praise for space and so much more.
For the neighbors we will meet
For the food we here will eat.
Praise you, Father, Praise you, Son.
Praise you Spirit, for our home.

God, your thankful people come
Giving you this special home.
Take the title that we bring.
Let our honest praises ring.

This is also your new home,
Welcome, Lord, to all we own.
Praise you, Father, Praise you, Son.
Spirit, come, dwell in our home.

8. Brunch

FRUIT BASKETS

Select large oranges or grapefruit with
not-too-thin skin. Cut fruit in half, and
remove segments. Save shells.

Section all the fruit, removing seeds
and pulp. Mix with other fresh or canned
fruits, and place fruit back into the
basket shells. Chill. Just before serving
sprinkle each shell with ginger ale and
top with nuts; garnish with washed mint
leaves.

SANDWICH LOAF

Serves 10-12
1 loaf unsliced bread
butter
2 large packets of cream cheese
3 Tablespoons milk
ripe olives
pimento
parsley
watercress

Remove crusts from bread and cut into
4 slices lengthwise about 3/4 inch thick.
Spread 3 slices with butter. Place one
slice on platter or board. Top with tuna
spread. Spread two of the remaining
slices, one with ham spread and the
other with cheddar cheese spread.

Reassemble loaf, cover with a damp
towel, and chill.

Before serving, frost with cheese
frosting. Beat cream cheese and milk

until it reaches a frosting-like consistency. Spread on sides and top of chilled sandwich loaf. Decorate with olives, pimento, parsley, and watercress. You might make a little flower design using the pimento as the petals. Chill until serving.

TUNA SPREAD

1 large can of water-packed tuna
mayonnaise
5 green olives
Cut olives into little pieces. Mix all ingredients, adding mayonnaise until a good spreading consistency is reached.

HAM SPREAD

1/2 cup shredded Swiss cheese
1 small can of deviled ham
1 teaspoon minced onion
1 Tablespoon sweet pickle relish
1 Tablespoon finely chopped green pepper
1/2 teaspoon nutmeg
When Swiss cheese has come to room temperature, add ham spread, onion, pickle relish, and green pepper. Beat.

CHEDDAR CHEESE SPREAD

1 1/2 cups shredded cheddar cheese
1/4 cup milk
1/4 teaspoon Worcestershire sauce
1/2 teaspoon curry
2 Tablespoons chopped ripe olives
Allow cheddar cheese to come to room temperature. Add milk and Worcestershire sauce; beat until smooth. Stir in olives.

If you have a large number of children, you may want to age-grade the food! For example, corn puppies might be a lot more popular than a sandwich loaf.

CORN PUPPIES

1 pound frankfurters
1/2 cup catsup
1/2 cup crushed corn flakes
Cut the frankfurters into bite-sized pieces and roll them in catsup and corn flake crumbs. Bake in 350° oven for 15 minutes.

Or use mustard instead of catsup.

SPAM SPECIAL

Spam sliced
brown sugar
ginger ale
Sprinkle spam slices with a small amount of brown sugar, nutmeg, cinnamon, and ginger ale. Place in a 350° oven and bake until brown. Serve on buttered whole wheat toast.

CHOCOLATE SCOTCHAROOS

1 cup granulated sugar
1 cup light corn syrup
1 cup peanut butter
6 cups Rice Krispies
1 cup chocolate drops (or butterscotch drops)
Combine sugar and corn syrup. Place over moderate heat until they boil. Stir constantly. Remove from heat and add peanut butter. Stir. Pour mixture over Rice Krispies. Pat into buttered pan approximately 3/4 inch deep. Cool. Melt chocolate drops (or butterscotch drops) and spread on the top.

SOME ADDITIONAL
HOUSE DEDICATION IDEAS
Choral Reading
Why not develop a Scripture choral reading that will involve both the family and guests? (See pages 107-111 for more ideas on how to write a choral reading.) This could be part of section 7—Vows of the Family.

Here are a few lines to show you what your finished reading might look like. All references are from *The Living Bible*. I changed the pronouns from I to we when the group was speaking. The references should not be read as part of the reading.

All: We will sing about your loving-kindness and your justice, Lord. We will sing your praises!

Family: We will try to walk a blameless path, but how we need your help, especially in our own home, where we long to act as we should (Psalm 101:1, 2).

Father: Decide today whom you will obey.

Family: But as for us and our family, we will serve the Lord.

All: Yes, we choose the Lord, for he alone is our God.

Pastor: You have heard yourselves say it. You have chosen to obey the Lord.

All: Yes. We are witnesses.

Family: Yes, we will worship and obey the Lord alone. (Sections from Joshua 24:15-24.)

Guest 1: Continue to love each other with true brotherly love. Don't forget to be kind to strangers, for some who have done this have entertained angels without realizing it.

Guest 2: Honor your marriage and its vows, and be pure.

Guest 3: Share the sorrow of those being mistreated, for you know what they are going through (from Hebrews 13:1-4).

Guest 1: God has given each of us the ability to do certain things well. If your gift is that of serving others, serve them well. If God has given you money, be generous in helping others with it.

Guest 2: Don't just pretend that you love others; really love them. Love each other with brotherly affection and take delight in honoring each other.

Guest 3: Be glad for all God is planning for you (from Romans 12:6-12).

Family: But as for us and our family, we will serve the Lord.

All: But as for us and our families, we will serve the Lord.

Symbolic Gifts
In a home where there are children, a symbolic gift can take on great significance. As the parents and children prepare the gift before the house dedication and then share with the guests what it means, they are underlining in the minds of their children that this house does indeed belong to God. The symbol will remain on display in the home —daily bringing to the children's and parents' minds the vows they took.

Here are some symbol possibilities. Put the pieces together and add your own touches.

Rocks—these can symbolize both the home and the fact that the home is founded on Christ Jesus, our Rock.

Homemade wooden cross—a reminder of the sacrifice Christ made for us and how little the sacrifice of our home is by comparison.

A collage of items belonging to each member of the family—perhaps arranged in the shape of your house. The center could be a picture of Christ. Baby could contribute a rattle. The school age child might give a well-done school paper. The toddler might add a crayoned picture. Mother might add something important to her. For example, I would add a pen since I spend most of my free time writing. Father would do the same. Jack might add some swatches of his favorite wallpaper as an indication of his excitement about making the house beautiful. All these could be glued inside a house frame to make an "US" picture.

The family could make a family flag.
Use the coat of arms and add some special indication of the King to whom the family belongs. The family might actually want to fly the flag on special days: birthdays, holidays, and the yearly anniversary of the home dedication.

A Gift from the Guests
It might also be appropriate for the guests to present the family with a symbolic gift.

At Gil and Ruth's house dedication, we brought a small tree to plant in their yard. We told them that we wanted their home to grow in all the special personal ways a living home can grow. As they watch the growth of our little tree from year to year, they will be reminded of how good God has been to provide for their needs and how much they have grown in their love for each other and for him.

OTHER SYMBOLIC GIFT IDEAS:
A lovely picture frame, probably 8" x 10". Specify that the frame should be refilled each year with a picture of the whole family inside or outside the home. It will serve as a visual reminder that they are together for a purpose. God planned them, and they are very important to him.
A jar or can of fruit from each person present. This is a symbolic picture of the fruit that this family can potentially bear as they all live for Christ in their community.
A large, homemade card on which everyone present has written a prayer.

FAMILY COMMUNION
"Remember Me Until I Return."

Objective: A Christian family (or group of two or three families) will remember Christ's death and resurrection by holding a communion service.

Basic idea: A celebration of communion will be held in the home. This allows parents to talk with children about what the elements mean, and allows the children to ask questions. It also provides an opportunity for a meal together, followed by some family praise games.

This communion service is designed to take place in the home with the head of the household taking the lead. Some people are uncomfortable celebrating communion without the pastor leading. If you are, why not invite the pastor and his family to share the experience with you. Let him offer the elements while you take responsibility for the rest of the evening.

What you do will depend on the ages of your children. But this outline could serve as a starting point:

1. Preparation—the night before
2. Sing resurrection songs
3. Share a Christlike action
4. Talk about the purpose of the Lord's Supper
5. Spend time in private prayer
6. Participate in taking the elements
7. Serve someone else a meal
8. Play a praise game
9. Again sing resurrection songs

If you allow 45 minutes for the meal, the entire communion evening will run about two hours for a six-member family unit.

1. Preparation—the night before
Explain what will be happening. Make certain everyone has cleared his schedule. Encourage young people to approach this evening with anticipation.

If you have junior or older aged children in your home, involve them in all the planning, including the preparation of the meal.

Each person should come to communion time with some special offering of himself—something that expresses that person's love and thankfulness to Jesus.

Parents will need to help younger children. Don't force great significance into what they do. A simple scribbled picture from the four-year-old to Jesus might be just as meaningful at his stage of development as a praise poem or

original song would be to you or your teenager.

THE EVENING
2. Sing resurrection songs
In communion we are remembering Christ's death—that horrible, painful expression of his total love for us. And we are also remembering that he is coming again. Begin by singing songs that focus on the joy that lies in our understanding of communion. These could be favorites suggested right now or the choices could be made at the planning the night before. Songs could include "Christ the Lord Is Risen Today"; "Up from the Grave"; "For God So Loved the World."

3. Share a Christlike action
Christ has made some differences in our lives, and if we are growing to be more like him, those differences between us and non-Christians are growing daily too. Ask the family to share some positive thing in their lives which emphasizes to them, and perhaps to others, that they are growing.

You may need to help young children with a few leading questions. "How did Jesus help you today?"

An elementary child might say, "I didn't cry today when I was scared. Instead I remembered that Jesus is with me."

An adult might say, "I actually witnessed today. This guy at the office asked if church was just a social deal for me or if I really believed what they were peddling. I honestly opened my mouth and told him what God meant to me."

4. Talk about the purpose of the Lord's Supper
In this section, involve everyone in questions and answers. Here's where you have the opportunity to train your young people, to guide them toward a greater understanding of this ordinance than they could ever get in an all-church explanation of the Lord's Supper.

Read 1 Corinthians 11:23-31 aloud. You may want to use a modern version or a paraphrase of this familiar text. Allow your voice to pick up the expression you think the early church leaders might have used when they read these commands.

Here are some questions about communion that have been arranged by age levels. Pick those which seem best for you and your family group. Don't use all the preschool questions at one time and then go on to another age level. Intersperse them so the whole family will be participating together.

Preschool:
How do you know that Jesus loves you?
What is a story about Jesus that you want to remember forever?
Would you lead us in singing "Jesus Loves Me"?
Who else in this room do you think Jesus loves?

Note that none of these questions calls for any symbolic understanding on the part of the child. If he has grown up in a Christian home, he knows Jesus loves him.

In some cases, the preschool child may have made a personal commitment to Christ as Savior. In many cases, that decision will come in the next few years. Right now it is important that he feel included in the family—included in this very special event that will have deeper significance as he matures.

Younger elementary children:
Are you sure that Jesus still loves you even when you're bad? How do you know?
Will you tell us the story of Jesus' dying on the cross?

Here you may have to help the child, but allow him to fill in the blanks so he gets a feeling of story participation. For example, you might say, "Jesus and his disciples were in a garden. Jesus was praying when all of a sudden...what happened?"

Can you tell us why Jesus had to die on the cross?
What do we mean when we say we are going to have communion?
Tell a reason why you love Jesus.

If you are certain the child understands what Jesus has done for him and has personally accepted him, you may ask the child to tell how he knows that Jesus lives in his life. Or if his salvation experience was expressed in public, you may ask him to share what he did and why.

Older elementary children:
Usually when we have communion in church we just have a swallow of juice and a small piece of bread. So why do we call communion "The Lord's Supper"?
Can you tell us the story of Jesus' eating his last supper with his disciples, the night he gave them the communion service as a way of remembering him?

136

If the child is a good reader, you might ask him to read Matthew 26:26-29 and Mark 14:22-25.

Kids your age usually aren't perfect. What are some of the sins of people your age that Jesus died to take away?

Suppose we had a visitor at our church on Communion Sunday. She asks you if she should take it. What would you say?

All Others:

What is a symbol? What does communion symbolize? (Or if you prefer, what do the bread and wine become when we participate in communion? What makes this important to us?)

If you were going to explain communion to a very young Christian, what would you say?

This will recap what others have said. That's good. The question forces people to think what they believe and state it without the clichés that so often limit our conversation with non-Christians or new Christians.

What areas in your life are you interested in giving more fully to Christ? (Do not assign this question. Allow volunteers to answer.)

Share how you felt the first time you took communion.

What are some of the things that often make communion less special to you now than it was the first time? How can we bring new life into our personal participation of this living ordinance?

5. Spend time in private prayer

Each person should ask Jesus to clear his life of sin.

This is an important time, directly commanded by Scripture. To emphasize its importance, you may want to reread 1 Corinthians 11:27.

At the end of this time, play a recording of quiet meditation music.

6. Participate in taking the elements

There are a number of ways this communion can be served. Here are a few ideas that have been meaningful to me:

a. The pastor will serve the elements to each person. To each, he says something personal: "Marlene, this is Christ's body which he gave for your sins."

b. Bread loaf and juice are placed on the table. As each person finishes his prayer time, he rises and breaks off a piece of bread, eats it, and drinks from the cup.

c. Each person comes to the table and takes a piece of bread from the loaf. He breaks that piece in two and gives half to someone else in the group. He says something like, "I'm glad we can participate in praising God together." Or, "I'm glad we're family members—physically and spiritually."

At a small Sunday evening service at our church, our pastor led this type of service. Three people shared their second piece with me. I have rarely felt as affirmed and accountable for my growth as a Christian.

d. The head of the house will break off a piece of bread and serve it to the next person, saying, "This is my body, which is given for you." That

person will eat and then break
off a piece and serve the next
person. Each person is symbolizing
his commitment to Christ and to his
family members. The same process
can be followed with the passing
of the cup.

What about small children who up to
this point have been part of the family
celebration and who may now feel left out
because they are not yet aware of what
Christ has done for them.

Within a Christian family, it may be
perfectly fine for them to take a piece of
bread and a sip of juice. When they
are served, the person may say, "This
food (drink) is to help you remember
that Jesus loves you. Do you love Jesus?"
When the child answers, he is allowed
to partake. For those who see communion
as symbolic, the leader's words have
changed the meaning of the symbol for
the child into something concrete that he
can understand and affirm.

Or you may want to have special food
for the children. Perhaps cookies and
milk. Explain that they are to eat and
drink slowly, and try to think as they eat
of all the reasons why they love Jesus.

7. *Serve someone else a meal*
Why not plan a love feast—a meal in
which the conversation is structured so
that Christ is the focal point. Work to
avoid the trap the early Christians fell
into. Remember Paul's scolding? "When
you come together to eat, it isn't the
Lord's Supper you are eating, but your
own. For I am told that everyone hastily
gobbles all the food he can without
waiting to share with the others."

Place a simple supper on the table.
Each person should serve the person
next to him. This will be difficult for small
children, but help them. Everyone
should understand that what they are
doing is a symbolic picture of what Christ
expects them to do all the time—think
about others first and show love to
them, just like Christ showed love to us.

You may want to set a chair at the
table to visually represent Christ's
presence at the meal.

After everyone is served, the head of
the house should direct conversation. At
this meal, everyone is going to talk
about things that point to our love for
Christ or the things that make us special
because we have accepted his love.

I've supplied some topic ideas. In some
cases, it will be hard for young children
to participate. Make certain that each
is asked to give some comments often
enough to allow them to feel a part of the
conversation.

Be careful, too, not to cut off conversation because it doesn't fit the list of
topics you've supplied. Your goal is to
have Christ glorified by the conversation
at the table. If that goal is being met,
don't worry about your topics.

Topic ideas:
Talk about all the special things God
has done for our family this year.

Talk about some of the good things
that have happened at church.

Share some of the dreams you have
for the growth of the family and the
children around the table. Be careful
not to embarrass anyone. For example,
I might share with my third-grade
nephew David, "David, this year I hope

you'll learn to read so well that you'll be able to read some of the stories about Jesus directly from your Bible. Wouldn't that be exciting?"

What are some of the things that make our family different because we are Christians? What are some of the things we should work on so it will be more obvious to others that we belong to Christ?

Talk about some of the problems that worry family members. Perhaps Mother could share her frustration with her job or a teen might share that he really needs prayer that he'll stick with algebra. Encourage everyone to accept these as "family" problems, not just the problem of the one member directly involved. Everyone should be aware of problems and provide prayer and personal support. (Note that this is not the time to talk about specific discipline problems.)

You might want to end the meal with the family singing a few of its favorite choruses or the first verse of several favorite hymns.

8. Play a praise game
Why not? Keep the games fun and encourage everyone to participate.

BIBLE CHARACTERS' PRAISE
Before the evening, cut out of paper at least twenty-five blocks that are big enough for people to stand on. Number them in order—1, 2, 3, and so on. Color two or three of the blocks.

Place the blocks in a line around the room. As people answer questions, they will move along the line, standing on the correct block.

You will need a spinner or a penny to tell each person how far he moves on each turn. For example, if the spinner goes to three, the person will move three blocks. Or heads could be two moves and tails one.

You will need to write some praise questions. I've gotten you started by writing ten questions, but you'll need about twice that many.

The object of the game is to be the first person to get through the twenty-five blocks.

If that doesn't seem like a long enough game, make the winner the first person to go through the blocks twice.

People are to stand on their blocks. If they answer their questions correctly they are to move ahead the number indicated on the spinner. If they miss, they move back the same number as the spinner indicated.

When a person lands on a colored block, he is given a personal question rather than a Bible praise question. I've given you several personal questions, but you will need to develop others. When you have prepared this game, it will truly be your family's original!

PRAISE QUESTIONS—the head of the house will ask questions and not participate in the game.
(All these questions are built around people in the Bible who had reason to praise God.)
  1. What woman praised God for her new baby and later gave the baby to serve God in the Temple? (Hannah)
  2. Peter was walking on the water. Suddenly he began to sink. Minutes later he was safe. What reason did

he have for praising Jesus? (Jesus lifted him from the water.)

3. A very smart sister saved her baby brother's life. Years later when the baby was grown he became a great leader. What was the baby's name? (Moses)

4. An angel told a woman she would have a special baby who would grow into a man who would save people from their sins. What was the woman's name? (Mary)

5. What a terrible rain! But the man in the boat and his family could praise God that they were safe. What was the man's name? (Noah)

6. The disciples praised God because his son had chosen them to be fishers of men. Name ____ disciples. (Adjust the number of disciples to the capabilities of the person who gets this question.)

7. A lady was very old and she still hadn't a baby. Then she had Isaac. What was the name of this lady who praised God for her miracle baby? (Sarah)

8. What special reason did Cornelius have for praising God? (His family wasn't Jewish, yet God made it clear that everyone would be included in

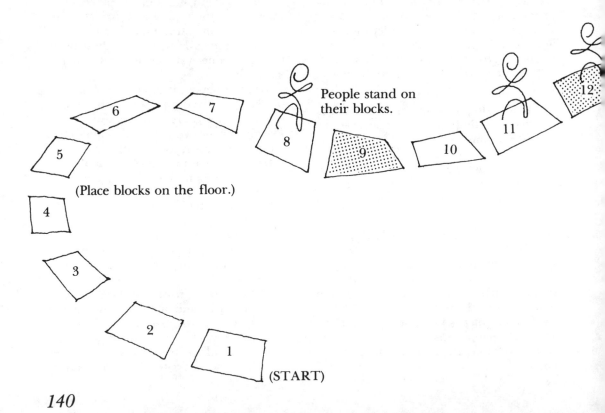

People stand on their blocks.

(Place blocks on the floor.)

(START)

Family Communion

his new family.)

9. What prophet didn't praise God when God saved a whole city through his preaching? (Jonah)
10. What book of the Bible is filled with songs of praise to God? (Psalms)

Now you're on your own. Write some more praise questions. They're fun and easy—and also a great way to involve your young people in the planning for this evening.

Colored blocks:
When a person hits a colored block, he has to answer a personal praise question. Or he can say, "Pass," and miss his next turn.

Here are some personal praise questions. You will need to write more. Keep them fun and light.

1. Name one thing you should praise God for this week.
2. Spell the word praise backwards.
3. Tell why praise is such an important part of the life of Christ.
4. What does the word praise mean to you?
5. What happens when a Christian neglects to praise God?

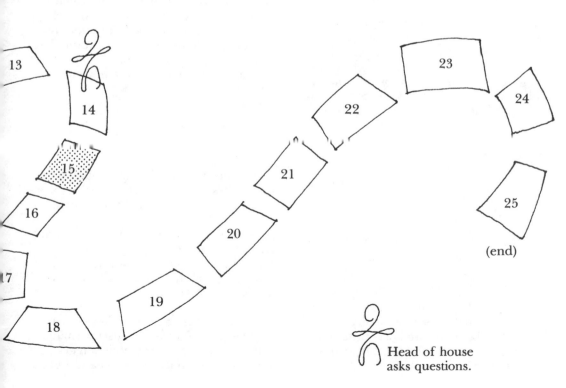

(end)

Head of house asks questions.

9. Again sing resurrection songs
Re-sing some of the songs you sang earlier. Between songs, each member could present to Jesus in front of the group the special offering of himself that he prepared the night before.

Optional:
If most of your family is ten years old and older, you might want to end this family communion evening by writing and reading acrostic prayers. In an acrostic, you start with a key word. In this case you would want to pick the word PRAISE that has been key throughout the evening. Each person writes a praise-prayer sentence or phrase for each letter in the word.

I've enclosed my example. You might want to do one for your family to give them an idea of what you mean. This is a special poem to God. If someone can't think of something to say about one letter, he should just move on to the next one. No one has to finish. When a few minutes of writing have passed, each person who wishes should pray aloud what he has written.

P—Praise you, God, because you love me,
R—Really love me enough to send Jesus to die.
A—Am I thankful to you?
I—I sometimes forget to say it, but I am.
S—So hear my poem of praise tonight.
E—Each day help me remember to tell you I love you.

This whole service is aimed at the Christian family. However, many families have members who are not committed to Christ. Should they be left out of this family time?

My opinion is that they should be told exactly what will happen and be warmly invited to participate as fully as they can without violating the rules God placed on communion.

For example, they might enjoy the resurrection songs. They might be able to answer some of the communion questions that do not require personal answers. They would enjoy the meal and perhaps the game. Do everything possible to help these people not feel like odd-people-out.

If a non-Christian comes, don't adjust any of your responses to fit what you think he needs to hear. This evening is for Christians. Don't feel obligated to present the entire plan of salvation complete with invitation. That not only limits the effectiveness of the communion time for the Christians, but it may offend the non-Christian family member who has agreed to take part.

PROGRESSIVE HOUSEWARMING

Goal: The church will "warm" the homes of families who have just moved to new houses or recently joined the church.

Basic idea: Church members will visit at least three homes of people who are part of the church and eat one course of a meal in each home. The guests will supply the food.

Several months ago, our home was the middle part of a three-house warming. Each of us in the three houses had recently made our purchases and were

INVITATION IDEA

A PROGRESSIVE HOUSEWARMING

Appetizers at _____
Main Course at _____
Dessert at _____
R.S.V.P. with the dish you will bring.
Time:
Date:
Optional Warming ideas:
A homemade warming card for each house
A warming plant for each house
A warming can of soup for each house

still in the process of moving in. Our guests were Christian friends who wanted to see our homes and welcome us into our new surroundings.

People signed up to bring an appetizer, main course, or dessert to one of the three houses. This took care of the food and left the new homeowners free to take care of unpacking and house-cleaning!

Under no circumstances try to make this progressive housewarming a surprise for the families.

When people came to our house, I was ready. There was still a hole in our front porch step, the bottom pane in the storm door was missing, and there were no lights in two of the upstairs rooms. I didn't mind; those just happened to be areas we hadn't gotten to yet.

But because I knew people were coming, I had time to clean the place and put the unpacked boxes into neater piles. There were so many people that they had to sit on the rug. It was comforting to know that no one would have to be drycleaned after the party!

Because I knew of the warming, I also had time to buy a mum and put it in our rather empty family room. I don't think too many people noticed or cared that it was there, but it was good for me. That flower said that the evening was special. I didn't have to apologize for what wasn't done yet. The flower announced, "Look folks. I'm blooming. Have a good time at the housewarming, because we're prepared!"

There was one room that had become the junk pile to top all. We hadn't done anything there at all. I put a big purple note on the closed door begging people not to enter that room. The note was laughed at and a lot of people threatened to peek, but as far as I know, no one did!

We started our Progressive House-warming at the condominium of a young couple who had recently moved from the south. Very few of us knew them well before the evening.

As people arrived, the hostess gave guided tours through the home, and the host made sure everyone had appetizers. The tour was fun. The hostess not only told us what each room would be, she also shared history on some special pieces of furniture and some great garage sale finds. I came away from appetizers feeling like I knew this couple a lot better. I could place them in their surroundings, and understood a little about their life style choice and values.

The main course was at Jack's and my home. It was fun to greet all the people who came—thirty or forty, I think. It was a warm feeling to know that they had cared enough about us and the others on the new house list to take a whole evening from their busy schedules to help us celebrate. This may have been the first evening I really felt at home in our new house. It was so much bigger than our apartment and so unfinished. I had longed to go back home—back to the apartment. But this occasion, along with our house dedication, made the place mine. I think we'll stay!

At each home a friend of the host couple had been asked to pray. Gladys prayed for our home:

Peace be to this house and to those who dwell in it. Peace be to those who enter, and to those who go out from it.

Almighty God, bless and hallow this house, this home, so that by your power and love it may be for Marlene and Jack a pure and happy place of shelter from the storms of life, and of provision for their needs of body, mind, and soul.

O God, whose Son for thirty years made his home with us, enable Marlene and Jack, taught by him, to live together in loving kindness, peace, and prayerfulness. May their home always be a dwelling fit for your presence.

Protect them from disease and privation, from calamity and accident, from fire, flood, and all perils of the elements and from the violence of men.

Let this household, O Lord, be ever linked with the household of faith, ever receiving the inspiration of Christian fellowship, and always open to those in need. Let others come here freely for love and understanding, and let your love radiate joy and peace from within its walls.

Come into this house, Lord Jesus. Dwell here, our Savior and Lord, forever and ever. Amen.

The warmers of the new homes may want to leave a personal note at each place. A homemade card is an excellent idea. A can of soup, a symbol of warm hospitality, is also a good idea. Or how about a plant, a symbol of growth?

The final course in our housewarming was at the home of a single parent and her sixth-grade daughter. It was great to see how Cathy, the twelve-year-old, became part of the whole celebration. She gave tours, spending lots of time showing her new pink bedroom. I think that during dessert she was feeling what I had felt during the main course—warm feelings that occur when a person knows her house is becoming a home.

7

SPECIAL HOLIDAY CELEBRATIONS

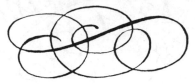

INVITATION IDEA

NEW YEAR'S EVE
DINNER AND WORSHIP

Dinner: 9 P.M.
Where:
After dinner, help plan a worship celebration
to God. Over the New Year's Hour, we
will present our worship to him.
Worship Planning Groups (choose one):
1. Praise to God for years past
2. Praise to God for this year
3. Praise to God for years to come

148

NEW YEAR'S EVE DINNER AND WORSHIP

Objective: A few adult members of the church family will meet in a home to have dinner together. After dinner, they will divide into task groups to plan a worship service. Over the midnight hour they will all participate in praising God through the service they planned.

Basic idea: A group of from ten to twelve people will plan their own worship service around the theme: Father, we praise you for our years—those past, this year, and the years to come.

I thoroughly enjoyed our New Year's Eve worship celebration. It had just the mix of worship and participation that I had been looking for.

I grew up attending watch night services at my church. I dreaded them. They included several Christian films, the annual report, a short punch and cookie break, and a long prayer time as we brought the new year in. It was a sitting marathon. I had no feeling of personal participation, of being involved in praising God for the new year. The quiet, and the people hedging my right, left, front, and back boxed me in.

Of course, many of my friends celebrated New Year's in a totally secular way. Jack and I were in Mexico City on our honeymoon. New Year's Eve fell on our fourth day together—a perfect opportunity to join in the world's festivities. We made 10 P.M. reservations at a French restaurant. The evening was awful. People were loud, slightly drunk, obviously determined to have a good

time. Everything seemed forced and phony. We finished our meal quickly and went back to the hotel. The secular celebration was no real option for me if I wanted to start the new year in a God-directed way.

After a lot of thinking, Jack and I came up with this party idea. It worked for us and the people in our church family. Would it work for you?

We invited thirteen people to our home for a late supper, followed by a planning time in which each of us contributed ideas on how we might praise God for the past, the present, or the future. When the worship planning was done—what songs we would sing, who would give testimony, etc.—we worshiped God together. Everyone was involved; everyone was praising God.

When Ken called to let us know he would be coming, he said, "I've had three other invitations, but this one sounds different. I've had it with New Year's, and your party just might revive my enthusiasm."

He and his wife came loaded with ideas to contribute to the worship planning. She had even brought her guitar and copies of new songs she had written for the occasion.

At 12:30 after our worship service ended in a song of praise, we all clapped in enthusiasm and excitement over our Savior. We had found a personal and Christian way to celebrate the New Year.

OUR PLANNING OUTLINE

Use our outline as a guide. Change it to fit your own personal New Year's celebration.

149

Invitations:

Send them by November 1. Limit the number of guests to the number you can serve in a single room. (If you have a very small kitchen and no dining room, line up card tables across the living room.) It's nice to have everyone eating the late supper around the same table; it added to our growing feeling of oneness as we worked together on our worship service.

For our celebration, we invited only people who were dedicated Christians. And we made a point of mixing single and married people.

New Year's Eve

8 P.M. People start arriving. Hors d'oeuvres and punch time.

9 P.M. Sit-down dinner.

10:30 P.M. One hour of planning for the worship celebration.

11:30 P.M. through the coming of the new year. The worship celebration.

Now let's look at the evening a little more closely.

8 P.M. People start arriving. Hors d'oeuvres and punch time.

HOT APPLE CIDER PUNCH
---

1 gallon apple cider
2 teaspoons whole cloves
3 cinnamon sticks
2/3 cup sugar
Heat all ingredients until boiling. Reduce heat and simmer until serving time—at least a half hour. Optional idea: Float whole oranges studded with cloves in the punch bowl.

RUMAKI
---

chicken livers (each liver will make
* 2 appetizers)*
water chestnuts (each chestnut will make
* 4 appetizers)*
bacon (each slice will make 2 appetizers)
Teriyaki Sauce (see page 118 for recipe)
toothpicks
Cut chicken livers in half and quarter water chestnuts. Pour teriyaki sauce over them and allow them to soak in the refrigerator for at least 6 hours. Drain.

Cut bacon slices in half and wrap a piece of liver and water chestnut in the bacon slice. Secure with the toothpick.

Place in the broiler until bacon is crisp, about 6 minutes.

STUFFED CAPS
---

mushrooms (each mushroom cap will be one
* appetizer; recipe adjusted to 1 pound of*
* mushrooms—about 25 caps)*
3 Tablespoons butter
1/4 cup chopped green pepper
1/4 cup chopped onion
1 1/2 cups soft bread crumbs
1/4 cup grated Parmesan cheese
1/2 teaspoon salt
1/2 teaspoon thyme
1/4 teaspoon pepper
1/2 cup chopped black olives
Wash mushrooms. Remove stems and chop them to add to the mushroom cap filling. Melt 3 Tablespoons butter in skillet. Cook and stir chopped mushroom stems, pepper and onions until tender. About 5 minutes. Remove from heat and stir in remaining ingredients.

Fill caps with mixture. Place mushrooms filled side up in a buttered baking dish and bake for 15 minutes. Then broil for about 2 minutes.

9 P.M. Sit-Down Dinner

This is a perfect occasion to get dressed up and eat a dinner that's a little more special than usual. You may want to do the entire dinner yourself, or ask others to bring certain dishes that will add to the festivities and participation. We chose to ask people to help. It was less money and work for us, and everyone seemed to enjoy preparing something for this evening.

JELLIED SALMON SALAD

3 cups canned salmon (water packed)
1 Tablespoon unflavored gelatin
2 cups hot water (use water from salmon pack)
1 Tablespoon finely chopped green pepper or
  parsley
1 teaspoon scraped onion
1 hard boiled egg, chopped
1 cup finely cut celery
shredded lettuce

Soak gelatin in two Tablespoons cold water for ten minutes; then dissolve it in the hot cups of water. When cool, add the rest of the ingredients.

Rinse individual molds in cold water and fill 3/4 full of the mixture. Set in refrigerator until firm.

Turn out on shredded lettuce and garnish with olives cut in rings. Put a dash of mayonnaise on each mold. Serves 6 to 8.

SUNFLOWER HAM CHICKEN

(12 servings)
16 skinned, boned chicken breast halves
16 slices of ham (thin)
1 cup salted sunflower seeds
4 cups herb seasoned stuffing mix
2/3 cup undiluted evaporated milk
2/3 cup melted butter

Flatten chicken breasts until 1/4 inch thick. Place each on a piece of ham. Combine sunflower seeds, stuffing mix, and evaporated milk. Mix well. Place equal amounts of the mixture on each breast. Roll and secure with toothpicks.

Place chicken and ham rolls seam side down in buttered baking dish; brush tops with butter. Bake at 350° for 50 minutes. Brush several times with additional butter.

Remove picks.

GOLDEN HEART CROQUETTES

(12 servings)
12 small carrots
2 1/2 cups cooked beef or veal
1 large can drained peas
1 medium onion
1/2 teaspoon salt
1/4 teaspoon nutmeg
1/4 teaspoon pepper
1 teaspoon Worcestershire sauce
2 eggs
2 Tablespoons water
1 cup fine dry crumbs
vegetable oil for deep frying

Cook carrots in salt water until tender. Drain.

Put meat, peas, and onion through the fine cutter of a food grinder. Add seasonings and 1 egg, lightly beaten. Mix. Cover each carrot with this mixture. Form into croquettes.

Beat second egg with water. Drip

croquettes into the mixture. Then roll in crumbs.

Fill flat-bottomed saucepan 2/3 full with melted vegetable oil. Heat it slowly. When it will brown a bread crumb in 50 seconds, it has reached the correct heat (375°). Slide in croquettes. Raise heat for a minute to prevent cooling. Fry until rich brown. Drain on absorbent paper. Serve with white sauce or tomato sauce.

CINNAMON SWEET POTATOES

4^1/$_2$ pounds pared, diced sweet potatoes
2^1/$_2$ cups boiling water
3 teaspoons salt
Cover and boil slowly for 12 minutes or until tender. Do not drain.
Add:
8 Tablespoons brown sugar
1^1/$_2$ teaspoons cinnamon
2 cups evaporated milk
4 Tablespoons butter
Cook slowly, uncovered until sauce is thickened—about 5 minutes. Serve at once. Serves 12.

BANANAS FOSTER

6 firm bananas sliced in half lengthwise
3/4 cup butter
2 cups brown sugar
1 cup chopped nuts
dash cinnamon and nutmeg
French vanilla ice cream
Sauté banana halves in butter. Sprinkle brown sugar over them. If sauce is too thick, add a couple of Tablespoons of orange juice. Add nuts, cinnamon, nutmeg. Broil in oven for two minutes.

Place bananas and sauce over ice cream.

10:30 P.M. One hour of planning for the worship service.
HOST COUPLE'S PREPARATION
Read through the following material and decide what you want to use, change, adapt. As people call to say they will be coming, explain a little of what you have in mind. Each person will choose if he wants to praise God for the past, the present, or the future. In fact, as people call, they may want to decide immediately what group they will be part of. In this way, they could be thinking about some songs or praise ideas that would fit with their group.

For example, a woman chooses to be on the team to praise God for the present —this year. This is the year the educational wing of her church has been completed and she has slides showing the progress. She brings along the slides and a projector and then with her group composes a praise prayer to read to God while the slides are shown to the whole party.

You will also want to have some supplies on hand that all groups can use: pad of paper, pencil, large sheets of paper, magic markers.

WORSHIP PLANNING
What does this term mean? Simply, each of the three groups will go through the process church leaders go through each week. They will pick songs that fit their aim. They will think of ways to involve the people from other groups. They will spend time praying about their part in the worship service.

I've suggested some ideas that would be helpful for each group. If groups are doing just fine without any outside help, great. Don't interject these ideas. But it's always good to have a few examples ready just in case the worship planning groups draw a blank.

Group 1: Praise God for the years that are past.
Theme: Father, we praise you for your direction over the years that are now past.

Get started by discussing how you could lead the other two groups in praising God for the years past.

What songs would be helpful? How about "God of Our Fathers"; "Rock of Ages"; "A Mighty Fortress Is Our God"? You might want to write the words on large sheets of paper so everyone will be able to participate in the singing.

Ask, "How can we involve others in the worship?" Perhaps you could ask for praise testimonies for specific things God has done in the past. Or you could ask people to share verses that have been meaningful to them in years past.

Could you develop a choral reading based on Scripture that would allow you to praise God for his past care?

Does the group have a sense of the dramatic? Perhaps you could begin with a roleplay between a Christian and a non-Christian. The Christian is telling the non-Christian why it's exciting to have God as a guide through his personal history.

Group 2: Praise for this year.
Theme: Father, we praise you for this year.

Get started by discussing how you can lead others in praising God for things he has done this year.

Could each person in the group give a three sentence overview of how God has guided his family this year?

Could the group develop a current events reading? One person would act as a newscaster reporting some of the key events of the year. Other people from the group would respond with Scripture verses showing God's control, or testify with personal affirmations that God has his hand on all of history and will control the eventual outcome.

Could you write some original words to a hymn or chorus that would praise him for this year?

For example, sung to *America,* the New Year's words in 1980 might be:

Guyana shocked us all—
The crime, the pain we saw.
We ask God why.
The graft in government,
The way the dollar went,
The bullets on killing spent:
Is life worthwhile?

We feel your presence near
Dissolving doubt and fear.
Help us to cope.
When evil seems to win,
Where God's love might have been,
We raise a banner over sin,
And claim God's hope.

Could you supply questions for discussion and ask the whole group to participate in grappling with the issues of the past year? For example:

In what ways are we Christians responsible for the government we have? In what ways can we have influence as "salt of the earth"?

Cults have been running rampant.

153

Secular sources are saying that these groups offer "family" to those who join them—something the joiners can get nowhere else. How do you think God wanted us to respond to this issue this past year?

What do you think was the event that most shook people's faith this year? How do we know God is really in control?

What about a prayer time in which people bring their current praises and concerns before God and the group.

Could the group plan a mini-sermon, giving illustrations from the lives of biblical people who praised God in the middle of terrible circumstances? For example, Daniel was dropped into the lion's den. David saw a lion charging his sheep. Peter stood alone in the crowd after denying his Christ. John was exiled. None of these people knew how God would use their terrible experience for his glory. But he did! Can we have that same assurance?

Group 3: Praise for the years to come. *Theme:* Father, we praise you for the future.

Get started by talking about what the world will probably be like in the next few years. How can Christians have total assurance that God is really in charge?

Select a few hymns or choruses that talk about the return of Christ. You may want to lead the whole group in singing: "This World Is Not My Home"; "Heaven Is a Wonderful Place"; "Blessed Assurance"; "Lead On, O King Eternal"; "Onward Christian Soldiers," and there are many more.

Could you lead a sentence round? The first person will start something about

his faith in God as controller of the future and others will add to that.

How about sharing a little about people who pointed you to Christ. Pick people who are now enjoying their futures forever with Christ.

In the worship, give everyone a sheet of paper. Ask each one to tear a symbol of his feeling as a Christian thinking about the future. Ask him to share what his symbol means.

11:30 P.M. through the coming of the new year. The Worship Celebration. Each group will lead the other groups in its part of the worship service.

Have a wonderful, Happy New Year!

At the end of our worship service, people immediately began talking about the next year. We decided that we would not get together in the same group again. Instead we would use what we had done in other New Year's Eve home celebrations and enlarge our circle of people who could participate.

This idea worked perfectly in the church we were attending because the church had decided not to plan a watch night service. A caution: The church is of primary importance in the growth of the Christian community. I think it would be wrong to plan a celebration like this one in your home if your church were also offering a special service. It's as if you're saying, "Don't go to church. We've got something better." Why not present this home celebration to your pastor and suggest that the whole church break up in homes across the community for smaller, less formal services. Divide the member-ship and regular attenders among the host families, and have a wonderful time praising God for the past, the present, and the security of our futures in him.

PASSOVER
An Easter Freedom Celebration

Goal: Families in the church will celebrate a Christian Passover. This celebration begins with the story of God's salvation for his people in Egypt and ends with our praise to him for our salvation through Jesus Christ.

Basic idea: Families of the church will follow some of the Jewish traditions associated with Passover, the most important Jewish festival of all. Christ's followers will discuss the Exodus Passover, celebrate a Passover meal, and conclude with a communion service. This should be a meaningful occasion, and a teaching opportunity for parents with young children.

WHO TO INVITE:
Why not divide the congregation into family groups? Host families will be responsible for inviting their assigned group to their homes. Portions of the meal should be assigned to each guest. Our church did this for several years, and it became one of our most meaningful traditions.

If the host families have small children, the meaning of the Passover can begin with the housecleaning for the event. Years ago, Jewish families combined housecleaning and the special cleaning for the festival which they called

Pesach (Passover). Walls were washed, furniture was scrubbed, and even clothes were given a good airing. All this was in preparation for remembering what God had done for his people.

WELCOME
The host should be in charge of the order of the service. Everyone is seated in the same room. Keep the seating arrangements comfortable, informal—no rows of chairs. In fact, it's appropriate if the small children are seated on the floor.

The host welcomes everyone: "Welcome to all who have no celebration at their home. Welcome to all who are hungry. Come and feast with us. Welcome to all who wish to join. Welcome as we look forward to the future and remember the past."

The host will fill a glass with juice or wine for each guest. Each one should take one sip. Then the host takes three matzos (unleavened bread available in most large grocery stores). Originally Jewish families took great pains to make this special bread from flour that had been harvested and milled under the watchful eye of the rabbi. The host should put these, one on top of the other, on a large plate and cover them with a napkin.

He then explains: "Matzo stands for unity. For Jewish people, the top matzo represents the priest. The middle one represents the Levite. The third one is known as the Israelites. Onc on top of the other, this bread symbolizes that all Jews are brothers.

"Can you tell me what the three pieces of unleavened bread might mean to us Christians here tonight?"

A young person could suggest that for Christians they might also stand for unity. All people who believe in Christ as their Savior are brothers and sisters in Christ.

The leader should then take the top piece and pass each around the group. Each person should break a bite-sized portion from the piece and eat it. He should then hand it to the next person saying, "I'm glad we're in the family of God."

THE STORY OF THE EXODUS
An excellent reader, chosen ahead of the Passover service, should read the story of the Israelites in Egypt. If there are a lot of children present, he may want to read the story from a Bible storybook. The story may be summarized from Scripture by reading Exodus 1:8-14; 2:1-10; 3:4, 7-10; 11:1-6; 12:1-14.

After the story has been read, the children participate in answering questions asked by the host. Here are some questions that might be helpful:

1. Why did the Israelites want to leave Egypt?
2. Why didn't the Egyptians want them to leave?
3. How did God help his people, the Israelites?
4. Why did God tell the people to celebrate the way they left Egypt for the rest of their life as a nation?
5. What are some special days Christians celebrate?
6. What does each mean?
7. What is the most important Christian holiday? (Easter) What happened on Easter?
8. On the Passover, we remember that God saved his people from slavery to the Egyptians. What did God save his people from on Easter?

THE SYMBOLS OF EXODUS
The host should now explain that the group is going to participate in a remembering celebration much like the celebration the Jews will be having on Passover. Each thing the group will eat points to something that they don't want to forget—and they don't want their children or children's children to forget.

Horseradish: The host should take the second piece of matzo and pass it with some ground horseradish. Each person should scoop a bit of the horseradish onto a piece of the matzo and eat it. He should explain that bitter horseradish is a part of the ceremony to help the people remember the bitterness of slavery and life in Egypt. The Talmud says, "In every generation, every Jew should see himself as if it were he who was redeemed from slavery in Egypt."

The leader should draw a parallel between the bitterness of physical slavery and the spiritual slavery to sin.

Mixture of chopped nuts, apples, and fruit juice (or wine): The leader should point out that this mixture looks a little like clay. Perhaps he could ask a child what the Hebrew people were to remember when they saw the food that looked like clay. It symbolizes the bricks the Israelites made for the Egyptians when they were slaves. It is passed and each person takes a bite.

Cooked egg: The egg is broken into pieces and passed. As each person takes and eats a bit of the egg, he is to remember the sacrifices that were offered for sins in the Temple. The host should ask why Christians no longer offer sacrifices for our sins.

Salt water and parsley: The salt water represents the tears shed by the Jews when they were slaves, and the parsley represents the new life that God promises his people. Each person should take a bit of parsley, dip it in the salt water and eat.

Prayers and Singing

In the Jewish Passover celebration, the people sing thanksgiving songs to God. The Christians at this Passover should sing songs now about the joy of being Christians. People can suggest a few favorites.

Then the host should pray, thanking God for his great gift of freedom from sin.

Juice (or wine)

Now everyone takes another sip of the juice (wine). In the Jewish festival, four sips of wine are taken. No one knows why just four, but some people think that each sip represents a promise that was made to the Israelites when they were freed from Egypt. "I will take you out of the land of bondage." "And I will save you." "And I will free you from slavery." "And I will take you to be a chosen people."

The Meal

In a Jewish home, this meal is traditionally the best the family can afford.

Depending on your enthusiasm for Jewish cooking you may want to try some of the traditional foods like egg soup and matzo balls. You might want to have roast chicken or lamb as a main dish. Other traditional touches that you can pick up at most large grocery stores include figs, marinated herring, kosher pickles, bananas, honey, kumquats.

In a Jewish home, one of the young children hides the dessert. The father turns to the child and begs him to find the dessert. The child will finally agree if the father will reward him. The father and child banter back and forth and finally the father agrees—for the sake of dessert. The host family may want to play out this special drama to add some fun to the evening for the children.

The meal is concluded with everyone thanking God. You might want to write a prayer that everyone will read in unison.

Lord, we praise you for the way you took care of your people. The stories in the Old Testament are exciting and filled with examples of your power. But our favorite story is in the New Testament. It's the story of the Resurrection! You gave up your life to pay for our sins. But you conquered death and rose to life. You, Son of God, are our Messiah. We praise you. Amen.

Coins for Wheat

You may want to take an offering for people who need special help this Easter time. Young people should be encouraged to participate on their own in this part of Passover.

Open Door Ceremony

Explain that Jewish tradition says that Elijah visits the homes of Jews on this night. He opens the door and announces that the Messiah will come, the one who will lead the people to their homeland.

On this night more than any other, the Jewish people who do not believe the Messiah has come continue to pray that God will send him soon.

You may want to change this ceremony and invite the small children to participate. Explain that in several days, Christians will celebrate the raising of Jesus from the dead. Sing a celebration Easter hymn. Then ask the children to open the door and shout, "You are welcome in this house, Jesus."

COMMUNION

For the Jew who has not accepted Christ as Messiah, the celebration has ended. But for the Christian who knows that Jesus is the Messiah, the most important part of the celebration is still ahead. Communion! Through celebrating communion, Christians remember what Christ did for them, and they are reminded that he is coming again. They are looking forward to the Messiah's return.

Before you serve the elements, make certain children from grade five up understand this transition. You might explain it once and ask them to answer these questions which will require them to state their understanding of what you have said.

Why are we ending our Passover with the celebration of communion?

Why don't Jewish people who haven't accepted Jesus as Messiah celebrate communion?

What does Passover help us remember? What does communion help us remember?

What does the Passover look forward to? What does communion look forward to?

For communion, there should be one piece of bread left for Christians to break and pass. The final bit of juice in the glasses should be used. For unique ways of passing communion, see page 137.

LEAVING

Ask people to leave in silence (or children to silently go to bed). In this way their thoughts can remain more completely on what has happened at this Passover. They have been reminded of the things that God has done in the past, the sorrow of Christ's death for us, and the joy we can have because we know he will return for us.

RECYCLED CHRISTMAS PARTY

Goal: The church family will gather in a home to sing Christmas carols and get to know each other better.

Basic idea: The host family should invite church people to help trim their tree. Each person is to bring an ornament that has been made out of recycled material. Each person will judge all the ornaments, play a recycled game, sing Christmas carols, and get to know each other better.

INVITATION IDEA
Send invitation on recycled paper—old Christmas cards, backs of bread wrappers, soup label—be creative.

Why WASTE December (party date)?
Put your WASTE together in an artistic
*   form. Add a hook and come hang it on*
*   our Christmas tree. RECYCLE your junk!*
JUNK IDEAS: 8 used paper cups, painted
*   and strung together*
Christmas bells made from old juice cans
soda cap wreath
R.S.V.P.
You just might win a RECYCLED prize.

AS GUESTS ARRIVE

Take people's recycled oraments at the door. Put a number on each and hang it on the tree. Try to keep guests from knowing who brought which ornament.

You'll be amazed at the creativity some people will exhibit. At the recycled party where I was a guest, people made doves from soap bottles, geometric balls from old Christmas cards and last year's wrapping paper, and a hanging pants pocket starched and filled with straw flowers. Quite often all people need is the starter idea. You've given them that with the recycled theme; don't be surprised if this party turns into a lot of fun.

At this party, like most others at which people are not all best friends, consider nametags. Why not make them before the guests arrive, out of all sorts of recycled material—similar to the materials you used for the invitations? Each tag should be original and different. This will add a festive start. For example, you could take the Styrofoam base under some vegetables you buy in a grocery store and write people's names on it. Decorate the base with last year's Christmas cards, colorful celophane from around candy and gum, and who knows what else! I'd start my collection of potential recycling material (nifty word for junk) about three weeks before the party. It's not hard to put together dubious works of art when you have all the materials in front of you.

After all guests have arrived, give each a ballot and ask each to vote on the ornaments now on the tree.

_____ *The most creatively recycled ornament*
_____ *The most amazing recycled ornament*
_____ *The ornament that rids the world of the most junk*

Prizes should be fun. As you award them, explain why the prize qualifies as a recycled goodie. For example, I might recycle a half-burned candle. It just drops and drips all over the place. I burned it as long as I could stand all its ugliness in the living room, and I would be happy to recycle it into someone else's home.

Or I might recycle a packet of ten of Jack's favorite recipes. Actually, this is a pretty nice gift.

There are magazines on recycled paper and writing paper made from recycled materials. If you want to spend money on prizes, these are possibilities.

CAROLS

Do you ever get tired of singing Christmas carols? I don't. I love to sing them, and I watch for their first appearance with as much enthusiasm as I do my first spring robin.

So gather everyone around a piano or a guitar (or just someone who can sing on tune) and sing away. Supply books, if possible. This way you can sing more than the most familiar verses.

Intersperse the singing with readings. People might bring a funny or serious article to share with the group. *Reader's Digest* is a good source. Limit readings

160

to three or four minutes. What you are doing here is recycling stories that others have enjoyed—passing along enthusiasm about Christmas.

A grab bag might also help break up the singing time. Before everyone arrives put each name into a bag. About every four songs, blow a whistle, stop everything, reach into the bag, and pull out a name. That person should then answer a recycle question. Here are some questions that would be great for recycling:

Recycle the story about the best Christmas gift you've ever gotten.

Tell about something you've gotten secondhand that you just love.

If you could recycle an event that happened this past year, living it again this coming year, what would it be?

Recycle the first verse of a carol we've already sung this evening.

Tell about something in your house that you really do recycle.

Share the name of someone at our church who is really good at recycling his or her faith.

If you could recycle one year of your life, which year would you choose? Why?

RECYCLED GAMES

Both of these games grow from the same basic idea, so plan to use just one of them.

New Clothes for Santa

Save several weeks' newspapers.

Divide the party into recycling groups. Explain that Mr. and Mrs. Santa need new outfits, and each group will be recycling the newspaper to make these special costumes.

Each group should pick two people to dress. Provide no scissors. With only the newspaper, tape, pins, and perhaps some construction paper, the group must come up with a nifty outfit for the pair.

Why not award the winning group a pack of gum? Explain that the gum is new, but it can be easily recycled by sticking it on the bedpost every night.

Recycled Christmas Music

Divide the party into recycling groups —recycling objects into musical instruments. Explain that each group is to roam through the house picking up unique musical instruments. They are to use their voices and their homemade instruments to present a Christmas carol.

Ideas for the music instruments abound. For example, someone might fill glasses with different amounts of water, and try to get a tune by hitting the glasses with a pencil. Or someone could put waxed paper over a comb and hum through it. Or how about just getting a pan and a spoon and banging away?

Again, the award could be new gum just perfect for recycling!

I like these games because they force people to create something out of nothing. Nearly everyone enjoys participating in this type of foolishness, and is amazed by what his group produces—not always pleased, but always amazed!

Food

Christmas cookies. You could ask each

guest to bring eight cookies or you could supply them yourself.

FRUIT JUMBLES

1 1/2 cups sugar
1/2 cup shortening
3 eggs
3 cups flour
1 teaspoon vanilla
1 pound chopped dates
1/4 pound chopped walnuts
1 teaspoon soda dissolved in hot water

Mix sugar, shortening, eggs, flour, and vanilla. Batter will be stiff. Add dates and nuts. Mix. Add soda last.

Drop by teaspoons on greased cookie sheet and bake in a (moderate) 350° oven for 12 to 15 minutes. Makes 2 dozen or more cookies.

OATMEAL MACAROONS

1 cup shortening
1 cup brown sugar
1 cup white sugar
1/2 teaspoon vanilla
2 eggs
1 1/4 cups flour
1/2 teaspoon salt
1 teaspoon baking soda
1/2 teaspoon cinnamon
3 cups uncooked oatmeal
1/2 cup chopped nuts

Mix shortening, sugars, vanilla, and eggs thoroughly. Add sifted dry ingredients. Fold in oats and nuts.

Drop by teaspoon onto ungreased sheets. Bake 12-15 minutes in 350° oven. Cool for 2 minutes before removing from baking sheets. Makes about 4 dozen.

On a second mix, why not add a package of milk chocolate chips?

ORANGE COCONUT CRISPS

1/2 cup butter
1 cup sugar
2 eggs
1 teaspoon vanilla
1 Tablespoon grated orange rind
2 1/2 cups sifted all-purpose flour
1/4 teaspoon soda
1 teaspoon baking powder
1/2 teaspoon salt
1/4 teaspoon cinnamon
1/4 cup orange juice
8 ounces shredded coconut

Cream butter and sugar until fluffy. Beat in eggs, vanilla, and orange rind. Sift flour with soda, baking powder, salt and cinnamon. Add half the flour mixture, blending well. Add orange juice. Blend in remaining flour.

Spread coconut on wax paper or in shallow pan. Drop cookie dough (it will be soft) by teaspoonfuls on coconut. Roll in coconut, coating generously.

Place cookies 1 1/2 inches apart on greased cookie sheets. Bake at 375° for 15 minutes.

NEVER FAIL FUDGE

12-ounce can of evaporated milk
1/4 pound butter
4 cups sugar
12 ounces chocolate melted
4 heaping Tablespoons of marshmallow cream
chopped nuts (optional)

Place milk, butter, sugar in saucepan. Bring to a full rolling boil. Stir constantly. Boil for 5 minutes.

Remove from heat and fold in chocolate and marshmallow cream. Stir until blended. Add chopped nuts, if desired. Pour into greased 8″ x 13″ pan. Cool and cut into squares.

CHOCOLATE SANDWICHES

4 cups flour
1 1/2 cups butter
1/2 cup fine sugar

Mix and roll into five long rolls—about 1 inch in diameter. Wrap in wax paper and chill.

When chilled, slice into 50-cent-sized circles (1/4 inch thick), and bake for 10 minutes at 400°.

Spread half the pieces with chocolate filling and top with the other half to create chocolate sandwiches.

Filling:
4 squares chocolate
3 Tablespoons butter
3 cups powdered sugar
1/8 teaspoon salt
5 Tablespoons cream
1 teaspoon vanilla

Melt chocolate and mix all ingredients together.

ORANGE NUT BARS

2 cups flour
1/3 cup sugar
1/2 teaspoon salt
2/3 cup butter

Sift dry ingredients together. Cut in butter until size of small peas.

Combine:
1 slightly beaten egg
1 teaspoon vanilla

Add to flour mixture, stirring with fork until dough is moist enough to hold together. Roll out half of the dough on 13″ x 9″ piece of wax paper. Roll to

the edge of the paper. Invert into a 13″ x 9″ greased pan. Remove paper.

Roll out remainder of dough on waxed paper to a 13″ x 9″ rectangle; set aside.

Filling:
2 cups chopped nuts
2/3 cup sugar
1 Tablespoon grated orange rind
1 cup orange juice
1 Tablespoon lemon juice

Combine all ingredients. Spread over dough in the pan.

Place remaining dough over filling. Remove paper. Prick generously with fork. Bake at 375° for 25 to 30 minutes. Frost immediately after taking out of oven.

Frosting:
1 1/2 cups sifted powdered sugar
1 teaspoon grated orange rind
2 1/2 Tablespoons orange juice

CHRISTMAS
Ideas to Add to Your
Family Celebrations

Aim for the ideas in this section: To start you thinking about the importance of starting meaningful traditions in your own family at Christmas time (and the year round).

Traditions are very important in a Christian family. They tie us to our past and help us remember events and emotions that might otherwise be forgotten. They say, "We always do this together. We are a family."

Think about the days when you were a

child. What family traditions did you have —the things your family always did together? You could count on these things happening.

I think about Friday nights and lemon ice cream sodas. I'll never drink a lemon soda without remembering the nineteen-cent ones at Garvin's Department Store and my mother. Every Friday night, we would go to town, often with only fifty cents between us. We would wander through the stores and talk. During those adolescent years it was easier to tell her what I was feeling and what had happened at school while we window shopped. She would share things that happened to her at work and what her dreams for my brother and me were. We would never have talked like that if we had just sat down and said, "Now, we'll talk." That would have been too threatening for me. Those two hours on Friday nights were tradition for us. She's dead now, but I can still look back on our Friday night outings and remember some of the wonderful ways she mothered and guided me.

Family traditions. What helps you remember those years gone by? More important, what will help your children and your grandchildren remember?

Christmas is the easiest time of the year to start or improve traditions—but don't stop there. Traditions fitted anywhere into your year underline the word *family*.

For example, here are some traditions celebrated by families that I know. They don't fit into the holiday seasons, but they're great for pulling a family together.

First robin tradition. When someone in the family sights the first robin of spring, the rest of the family is alerted. The next free day is robin-picnic day —even if there is still snow on the ground. This family will have their picnic anyway—just don their coats and off they go. Spring is just around the corner.

Family flag traditions. Each person in the family has his own flag. On his birthday and special achievement days (he scores the winning point at the basketball game), his flag is flown.

Doll tradition. One mother with five daughters makes each girl a birthday dress and an identical dress for each girl's doll.

Cleaning bird tradition. To make housecleaning a little more fun, a mother hides a cloth bird. The small children clean until they find it. Then it is break time for milk and cookies before finishing their jobs.

Little traditions woven into the fabric of our lives! Begin to build traditions into your family's year. And start at Christmas. It may make a difference in the enthusiasm of those who participate, and more important, it may make a difference in your children's appreciation for family.

Every Christmas our whole family meets together—three brothers, their wives, their mother, and three young nephews. These little boys, David, Danny, and Douglas add a lot of life to the celebration, especially when we want to settle down and listen to the Bible story of the first Christmas before we open presents. Chairs squeak, wrapping paper crinkles as little hands squeeze.

We hear whispers of, "When can we open the presents? How much longer?"

"What can we do to make them as interested in the true meaning of Christmas as they are in their gifts?" Jack asked. And then laughingly he answered his own question. "Nothing!"

He's right; they are just young children. But we could do a lot to increase their interest in the Bible story and at the same time begin to grow their understanding of the Christmas message.

So we decided to make them part of the Christmas story, instead of just listeners. These next two ideas were our answer to a meaningful Christmas tradition. Each year we will work together to make the story of Christmas live for the adults and children in our family. No longer will we whip through the verses in a dash for the first package. The birth of a tradition is exciting. You hardly realize it's been born until you look back and know how much it means to you and look forward to next year with new anticipation.

Try our ideas, and add to them, making them your own.

CHRISTMAS STORY ENVELOPES

Aim: To involve everyone at his own age level in the retelling of the first Christmas story.

Basic idea: Before the family meets for Christmas present opening, write one question for each person who will be present. Put that question into an envelope with the person's name on it. Match the questions to the abilities of the person. For the non-reader, draw a little stick figure picture that will illustrate a part of the Christmas story. When you're all together, read the Bible story and stop at appropriate places to ask the questions. The child will tell the part of the story that his picture represents.

Here's what we did in our family. Since we have a wide age span, this script will give you an idea of how you might develop your own.

Bible Reader: Luke 2:1-7. (Encourage the person who reads to use a lot of expression. After he has finished the verses indicated, he should call on the person who will answer the questions.)

Envelope 1 for David, a third grader: If Joseph and Mary had come to your door and asked for a room, what would you have said?

Bible Reader: Luke 2:8-14

Envelope 2 for David's Daddy: Suppose you had been one of the shepherds. How do you think you would have felt when the angels came?

Bible Reader: Let's sing a Christmas carol. David, which one would you like to sing? (Again, involve the youngsters.)

Envelope 3 for Danny; he's four years old and doesn't read yet. In his envelope was this picture. The Bible reader asked him to explain the story.

Bible Reader: Luke 2:15-19

Envelope 4 for Grandmother: Pretend you are a shepherd on your way back from seeing baby Jesus. You meet a good friend. What do you tell him?

Bible Reader: Matthew 2:1-12

Envelope 5 for Aunt Thelma: God gave us a wonderful gift when he sent us his Son, Jesus. What gifts can we give to Jesus?

Envelope 6 for Uncle Marc: What makes Christmas so special for Christians?

Christmas Story Envelopes are fun and they involve everyone. Even the opening of the envelopes is part of the fun. No one really knows what part of the story will be inside.

These envelope questions were designed to make the story clearer to small children and to hold their interest, even in a room full of wrapped presents.

What if your family is older? The same idea will work but you'll need to age grade the questions.

For example, in a family of teenagers you might use questions like these:

Bible Reader: Luke 2:1-7

Envelope 1: You meet someone on the bus who is just about toppling over with Christmas presents. You start talking about the real meaning of Christmas, and he says he can swallow everything but the virgin birth. How do you reply? Explain why the virgin birth is absolutely essential to the story of Christmas.

Bible Reader: Luke 2:8-14

Envelope 2: If God were sending his Son into our world today, to whom do you think he would send his special announcements? Why?

Envelope 3: What do God's birth announcements tell you about him?

Bible Reader: Luke 2:15-19

Envelope 4: Next to your salvation, what would you say is the most exciting personal gift God has given you? Lead us in prayer, thanking him for his most important gift, and all the others he gives.

THE CHRISTMAS STORY A FAMILY PLAY

An easy way to involve the whole family in the reading of the Christmas story is to script it and assign parts.

When we did this in our family, we gave the younger child a picture to read. Note that the following sample has been written at the children's level. They should be totally involved with the tradition of sharing the true story of Christmas.

166

Characters:
Joseph—Father
Mary—Mother
Shepherds—youngsters
Angel: Grandmother
Inn Keeper: Uncle
    We adjusted the parts to the people at our Christmas celebration. You'll have to do the same. If you have a very small group, there is no problem with someone being assigned two roles.)

Daddy: I got an order from Caesar Augustus, the Roman Emperor. I am to return to the town where my family used to live in order to put my name on a tax list. I am a member of the royal line, so I had to go to Bethlehem in Judea, King David's ancient home. I had to travel all the way from Nazareth in Galilee.

Mother: I am Mary, and I went with Joseph. It was a hard trip because I was going to have a baby. When we got to Bethlehem, I knew that the baby was coming soon. Joseph and I looked hard for a room where we could stay.

Uncle: When Mary and Joseph asked me if they could stay in my hotel, I said no. I didn't have any more rooms. But I did let them sleep in my barn.

Mother: There my baby was born. It was a boy.

(If there is a small baby in the group, Mother could invite the younger children to wrap a blanket around the baby just as Mary did with her little newborn son.)

Shepherd (child who can read): I was a shepherd in a field outside the village, and I took care of sheep. It was a long, hard job.

Shepherd (child who is too young to read):
    (An adult may have to ask the non-reader to explain his picture and prod him until he shares the correct answer. Most children will know immediately what the next part of the story is.)

Child (divide the shepherd roles among the children who can read): Suddenly the one angel was joined by many, many others, and they all praised God.

Child: Come on! Let's go to Bethlehem! Let's see this wonderful thing that has happened which the Lord has told us about.

Mother: The shepherds came and worshiped the baby. It was wonderful of God to send them a special birth announcement for his Son.

Daddy: What a wonderful Heavenly Father we have. Let's sing a Christmas carol now to thank him for sending Jesus to earth.

CHRISTMAS TIC TAC TOE
A Family Bible Game

You'll need at least twelve people to play Christmas Tic Tac Toe, a game involving review of the Christmas story and praise to our Savior.

    Arrange your chairs like a Tic Tac Toe game—three rows of three chairs in each row. One person should sit in each chair.

Two players should stand in front of the chairs. Each player has six construction paper blocks in his hands. One person's

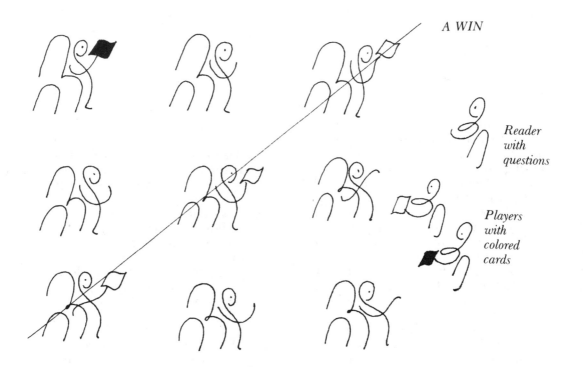

A WIN

Reader with questions

Players with colored cards

blocks should be red and the other's green.

Players should take turns calling on the people in the chairs to answer questions. They must call on someone before the twelfth person reads the question. If the person called on knows the right answer, the player gives him one of his cards to hold up. If that person doesn't know the answer, the next player takes his turn. The object, as in Tic Tac Toe, is to get three red or three green cards in a row.

Of course, children can play this game with adults. The person reading each question might adjust the difficulty of some questions for the younger children.

Make up your own questions for the game and build them all around the Christmas story. Here are a few to give you an idea. When all your questions are answered correctly, your family will have had an excellent review of the Christmas story.

1. Why did Joseph go to Bethlehem?
2. Who was the ruler at the time of Jesus' birth?
3. Why didn't the innkeeper take Mary and Joseph into his inn?
4. How many shepherds came to the manger to see Jesus? (Trick question. The Bible doesn't tell us.)
5. What did the shepherds do after they left the barn?

GOD GIFTS

Both children and adults can participate in this worship experience. Before the family opens its gifts, each person is given a colorful square of construction paper and asked to write or draw a gift on that square that he would like to give to Jesus this year.

Encourage adults to share what they are giving with another adult and ask that adult to hold them accountable to follow through on their gift. For example, I might draw a dollar sign and explain to my sister-in-law that I promise to give God 5 percent more money this year than I did last. She would check with me every once in a while to make sure that I was really doing what I had said I would do. Or she might write, "I will give my children to God by making a daily effort to teach them more about him." I, in turn, would check with her to see how daily devotions are coming and in what ways she is seeing their understanding of Jesus grow.

A young child's gift will have to be more immediate, something that can be done right now. For example, a child might draw a picture of himself talking to a friend and explain that later today when he goes over to visit Rodney, he will tell him about the true meaning of Christmas. Or he might write, "I won't fight with Susan today."

These gifts should be something you can measure. If the child doesn't fight with Susan all day, he has given Jesus the gift he said he would. I can measure the amount of money I give to God. My sister-in-law can plan for daily encounters with Jesus for her little boys, as well as using the spontaneous opportunities that come up during the day.

CHRISTMAS LIGHTS

After all the gifts are opened, each person takes a candle. The head of the home lights a large candle and places it in the middle of the room.

The leader explains that the large candle is a symbol of Christ, the light of the world. Our smaller candles represent us. Each person should take his unlit candle to the larger one and light his. In this way he is saying that he wants Christ to shine through his life; he wants to share his Christian light with others who are in darkness.

As each person lights his candle, he should share one way he has grown in his reflection of Christ this past year. Or, he could share one way he has shared his light with others.

After all candles are lit, the family might sing the doxology together.

This simple ceremony takes only a few minutes. It can be an excellent reminder to the whole family that this household is set apart by God.

GIFTS OF TIME

Each person will present a gift of time to other family members. What a difficult gift! It's not the type that can be purchased, given, and forgotten. This gift requires something of ourselves.

These gifts may be written or presented in the form of stick figure pictures. If the family is large, you might draw names and have each person give a gift of time to the person whose name he has drawn. This is an excellent tradition to start. If you do, stress creativity.

The first year, people may need some ideas. After that, they should do just great on their own. Here are some gifts of time.

I promise to vacuum the whole house every Tuesday after school throughout January and February.

I'm going to take you out to dinner with the money I make baby-sitting. Please save January 12 for the big event.

I promise to read you a story for fifteen minutes every night I possibly can for the next two weeks.

I will paint the kitchen and have it done by January 17.

I will save fifteen minutes talk-time just for you every evening right after supper.

I will help you with geometry until you bring your grade up to a B—even if it takes the rest of the year.

See? These are hard gifts, and I like them. Christmas is so much dumping of gifts all at once. Gifts of time force a family to think about what the other people would like to do. They stretch Christmas into the month of January. Gifts of time make me feel loved.

This parable might encourage your young people to try gifts of time:

TWO TREES
A Parable on Giving
The two trees winked at each other through the windows of their two houses. "You should see the stack of presents under me," bragged Spruce. "A red box, a huge green box, an enormous blue box, and a little silver box that looks

terribly expensive."

Pine smiled. "I've got envelopes under me," he said.

"What!"

"Yep!" Pine quivered his needles lightly. "I've got a white envelope, a tan one, and one that has little roses printed on it."

"How mortifying," Spruce sympathized. "Your family must be very poor. I feel sorry for you."

But Pine Tree only smiled.

Days passed and each day Spruce would report on the fine and wonderful additions under him. "Why, I'll bet it's going to take hours just to open all these gifts. And the wrappings. Why, they cost a fortune! I'm really impressed with Christmas in this house."

From his house across the street, Pine would share the growing number of envelopes, and Spruce couldn't help but hear the happiness in his voice as he reported.

"He's just hiding his embarrassment," Spruce thought. "Every Christmas tree's dream is to be filled to the boughs with presents."

The big day came. Spruce watched with pride as the children at his house whooped and hollered over their wonderful presents. One after another after another was opened. The beautiful paper was crumpled and thrown into a corner. And finally each person sat beside his huge stack of gifts. "They must be very happy," Spruce thought.

Then to his surprise he heard the girl say, "Is that all?"

"Yeah," the boy said. "Where's my bicycle? I wanted a bicycle. You never get me the stuff I want."

The girl grabbed a puzzle. "I'm going to put this together," she said.

"That's mine," screeched the boy and grabbed for the puzzle box.

"That's enough," the father shouted. "You ungrateful kids just get up to your rooms, and . . ."

More wails.

Spruce was flabbergasted! His branches dipped in sorrow and one glass ball slipped off and crashed to the floor.

"Isn't it awful," he said to Pine when the noise had cleared. But Pine was grinning. "Isn't your family screaming and hollering and fighting?" Spruce asked.

"No," Pine said. "First, they hugged. Then the mother and the oldest boy had happy tears running down their faces. Now they're eating dinner and talking about their gifts."

"What gifts? You just had envelopes."

"Yes, but in each envelope," Pine explained, "was a gift of time. Each person promised to do something nice for the other. Janet promised her parents she would make their bed every day in January. Robert promised Janet a trip to the aquarium and pizza afterward. The father promised the mother he would make windowboxes by spring and plant them with flowers. It was great fun opening the envelopes."

Spruce wiped the sap from his eyes. "I would give up all my tinsel if I could teach my family what your family knows."

FAMILY PROJECT

September is the time to start. Decide on a God Project to be completed by Christmas. Why not make it a big one —one that you couldn't possibly complete by yourselves. Then the family will have to depend on God's help, a very healthy dependence to build.

What is a family project? For you, I have no idea. It will be something done for the Lord. Usually it will involve money. Make it a rule that the money must be made for this project—no dipping into the bank account at the last minute to come up with promised dollars. Every member must contribute a fair share—a little for the young children and more for people who have more to give and more understanding of God's gift to us. No one should make up the part that another has promised to contribute. For example, if four-year-old Danny has offered to contribute one dollar, he will have to think of ways to earn it. If he doesn't, the project will be one dollar short; no one else can make up the difference.

Make sure the choice of the project is a family decision. Talk about what's involved and why the project makes sense. For example, if my family were picking a project right now, we might consider:

Buying a mule for Ed, a missionary friend in Mexico.

Sending Marian a $100 Christmas check to help with her work at the Japanese orphanage.

Donating a Mr. Coffee to the Community Center the church supports, and including enough money to pay for the first three months of coffee.

Sending Christian magazine subscriptions to fifteen retired people in our church.

All these projects are large and will take time and energy. What a perfect way to keep the truth about God's Christmas gift alive in the family.

How does a family earn money? Again, I have no idea. Each family will have different ideas, but the key word is creativity.

Have a garage sale, and tell everyone who comes where the money will be going. This sets the garage sale off as a type of mission project, too.

Use baby-sitting money to buy cake-making materials. Then have a cake sale in the neighborhood. Again, let everyone know where the money will be going.

Parents, make a list of extra chores smaller children could do that will allow them to earn a little money. These should be in addition to their regular responsibilities around the house.

Offer to scrape frost off neighbors' car windows before they leave for work; shovel snow; wash windows; change spark plugs.

There's no end to the list.

FAMILY REVIEW

Pick out six family slides for each of the last five years. Flash these on the screen as a review of each year. Then ask family members to think back and share what gifts God gave the family that year.

If possible, each family member should be pictured each year.

If we were doing this and the slides were flashed for 1978, the pictures might remind us to thank God for the gift of our old new home! We would thank him for Douglas, our new nephew. We would praise him for allowing Jack to have several very excellent free-lance decorating jobs.

Be as specific as you can.

Close the review and praise time with sentence prayers.

A FAMILY CAROL

Why not write your own family carol. It's not difficult, and it can be a great way to praise God.

Start with a favorite carol, and then work together to write new words to the familiar music.

It's not difficult for elementary children to help here. Each line should fit with the music; and it doesn't matter if the rhyme and meter aren't perfect. This will be a family song, and that makes even its imperfections perfect.

Our family might choose the "Away in a Manger" tune. See if you can sing our song:

1. Tonight in Oak Park, Lord, we pause before you
   To tell you we love you the whole year through.
   We thank you for Dougie, new baby this year
   And all of your gifts that have brought us good cheer.

2. We thank you for Marc and the new job he got,
   For Grandma who's fun and who loves us a lot

For Daddy and Mommy and
    presents tonight,
For aunts and for uncles to hold
    us real tight.

This is our special song because it
records events that are important to our
family. We could conclude it by singing
the real words to the song.

If the family started a tradition of
writing a family carol every year, it would
be fun to keep a record of them. As
the children grow, so may the selections
of family carols—each a unique praise
hymn to Christ on his birthday.

CHRISTMAS PICNIC

A family Christmas picnic is especially for
young children. The purpose of the
picnic is to capture for the children a
little of the feelings Mary and Joseph had.
Explain to the children a few days
before the picnic that the special day is
coming. Pre-arrange with a friend
(one the children know and like) that he
will tell you and your family that
there is no room in his house for you
when you knock on his door.

Pack a picnic lunch. Since much of the
world is cold around Christmas, this
picnic may be eaten in the car.

Explain that on this picnic, you will be
reviewing the wonderful Christmas
story. Don't tell the children where they
are going—only that it will be fun.
Stop the car about a mile from home, and
read the portion of Scripture in which
the census was ordered (Luke 2:1-5).

Then talk about where the children
think they are going. How do they feel
about the trip? How would they feel if

they were taking the trip outside in the
cold?

Move on to the friend's house.
Together go to the door with your picnic
things. Explain that you would like to
eat your picnic lunch with this person.
The friend should sadly shake his head
and explain that there is no room
for the family to eat in his house today,
but they are welcome to go out in the
backyard or garage to eat.

Parents should decide against that and
get back in the car. Read Luke 2:6, 7.
Ask children to tell how they felt
when the friend did not want them in his
house. Draw the parallel between
their experience and Mary and Joseph's
experience. How might Mary have felt?
What might she have said to Joseph?

Continue on your trip to a place
in the country where there are fields,
and if possible, barns. Stop the car
near a field and read the story of the
shepherds and the angels. See Luke
2:8-20. Talk about how the shepherds
might have felt. Could you all pretend
to be shepherds and hold a little
conversation such as they might have
held as they returned from seeing baby
Jesus?

Point to the barn, if there is one nearby.
Ask the children how they think Mary
felt about having her little baby in a barn.
If the youngsters think this is a great
idea, guide them in realizing how smelly
and dirty it was. Share the reason
God allowed his Son to be born on earth
—this was his way of telling us that
he loved us.

Finally find a nice place to park and
eat the picnic lunch. Talk about the rest
of this year's Christmas activities and

how they glorify Christ. Talk about why we give gifts and how much fun it is to give, as well as get, them.

On the drive home, sing Christmas carols.

SOME CHRISTMAS GOODIES

MINCEMEAT CAKE

1 cup mincemeat
1 cup chopped nuts
1 Tablespoon rum flavoring
1 teaspoon vanilla
1 cup mayonnaise
1¹/2 cup buttermilk
3¹/4 cup flour
1 teaspoon salt
1¹/2 cup sugar
3/4 teaspoon baking soda
grated rind of one orange

Combine mincemeat, nuts, rum flavoring, and vanilla. Blend in mayonnaise and buttermilk. Sift dry ingredients over mayonnaise mixture. Add orange rind and mix well. Stir in mincemeat mixture. Grease a tube pan. Place heavy brown paper on the bottom.

Pour batter into pan. Bake at 325° for two hours. Remove from pan and cool.

FUDGE CAKE

2¹/4 cups sifted cake flour
1 teaspoon baking soda
1/2 teaspoon salt
1 cup cocoa mixed with 1/4 cup water
1¹/4 cup milk
3/4 cup brown sugar
1 teaspoon vanilla
2/3 cup butter
1 cup sugar
3 eggs

Sift flour, soda, and salt together.

Heat cocoa and milk in saucepan until blended. Add brown sugar and beat until smooth. Mix in vanilla.

Cream butter with sugar.

Add eggs one at a time, beating well after each addition.

Add flour and chocolate mixtures alternately in small amounts, beating well after each addition.

Pour into 2 9-inch cake pans or 3 8-inch pans. Bake at 350° for a half hour to 35 minutes.

APPLESAUCE SPICE CAKE

1 package white or yellow cake mix
1 package small instant vanilla pudding
1/4 cup vegetable oil
1 cup applesauce
1/2 cup water or coffee
4 eggs
1/2 teaspoon nutmeg
1/2 teaspoon cinnamon
1/4 teaspoon pumpkin pie spice
1/2 cup chopped raisins

Combine all ingredients; mix well. Beat at medium speed for 4 minutes. Pour into 2 greased and floured 4" x 8" loaf pans.

Bake at 350° for 50 to 55 minutes, or until inserted toothpick comes out clean and cake pulls away from sides of the pan. Do not underbake. Cook 15 minutes. Remove from pans. Finish cooling on rack.

APPLE CAKE

2 cups sugar
1 stick butter
2 eggs
1 teaspoon vanilla

2 teaspoons allspice
1/2 teaspoon salt
2 teaspoons cinnamon
1 teaspoon baking soda dissolved in
   1 Tablespoon hot water
1 teaspoon baking powder
4 cups finely diced apples
2 cups sifted flour

Cream sugar and butter together. Add eggs and beat well. Add the rest of the ingredients. Add flour last, a little at a time. Put into an oblong 13 x 9 x 2 greased pan. Sprinkle with topping before baking. Bake at 350° for about 1 hour.

Topping:
1/2 cup brown sugar and 1 cup chopped nuts,
   blended together

CRUNCH CAKE

1 cup shortening
2 cups sugar
4 eggs
1 cup milk
11/2 teaspoons vanilla
2²/₃ cups flour
1/2 teaspoon salt
11/2 teaspoons baking powder

Topping:
1/4 pound butter
1/3 cup sugar
11/4 cup chopped nuts
1/4 pound crushed vanilla wafers

Crumble and mix all topping ingredients. Press them on the bottom and sides of a tube pan or 2 loaf pans.

Cream shortening with sugar. Add eggs and beat well. Add remaining ingredients and mix thoroughly. Pour batter into prepared pans. Bake at 350° for 1 hour. Can be glazed while warm.

PECAN PIE

1 Tablespoon butter
1 cup brown sugar
1 cup light corn syrup
3 eggs
1 teaspoon vanilla
1/4 teaspoon salt
1 Tablespoon grated orange rind
1 cup pecan halves

Cream butter and sugar. Add syrup, well-beaten eggs, vanilla, salt, and orange rind. Mix well. Add pecan halves.

Pour into a prepared, frozen crust.

Bake at 350° for about a half hour or until inserted butter knife comes out clean.

MINCEMEAT COOKIES

11/2 cup soft butter
3/4 cup granulated sugar
3/4 cup brown sugar
1 egg
1/4 cup milk
1 Tablespoon rum flavoring
41/2 cups sifted flour
3/4 teaspoon salt
3/4 teaspoon baking soda
2 cups mincemeat pie filling
1/2 cup orange marmalade

Cream together the butter (or margarine) and sugars until light and fluffy. Add egg, milk, and rum flavoring. Beat well. Sift together flour, salt and soda. Stir into creamed mixture.

Divide dough into half. Wrap and chill thoroughly.

On a well-floured surface, roll half the dough at a time into 1/8 inch thickness. Cut out cookies using a 21/2-inch cutter. Using a 3/4-inch cutter, cut a small hole in the center of half of the circles of dough.

Combine mincemeat and marmalade. Place two teaspoons of mincemeat mixture on each uncut cookie. Top with the cut-out cookies. Seal edges with a fork.

Bake on ungreased cookie sheet in a 375° oven for 10 minutes or until a light golden color. Remove cookies from the sheet while they are still hot. Makes 3¹/₂ dozen cookies.

FILLED COOKIES

¹/₂ cup shortening
¹/₂ cup sugar
1 teaspoon vanilla
1 egg yolk
1 cup flour
1 teaspoon baking powder
¹/₄ teaspoon salt
red jelly or other filling

Cream shortening with sugar. Add vanilla and yolk. Blend. Stir in dry ingredients. Blend. Roll into balls. Make depression. Fill before baking. Bake at 350° for about 10 minutes.

SOFT GINGERBREAD COOKIES

2 sticks margarine
1 cup sugar
1 teaspoon ginger
1 teaspoon cinnamon
¹/₂ teaspoon salt
1 teaspoon baking soda
1 cup molasses
2 eggs
4 level cups of flour

Cream margarine (or butter) with sugar. Add spices, salt, and soda. Stir in the molasses, and then the eggs. Blend in the flour 1 cup at a time.

Chill well, preferably overnight.

Roll a little at a time. For soft cookies, roll thicker. Bake approximately 12 minutes at 350°. Watch carefully so they won't get too done, or else they won't be soft.

MACAROONS

2 egg whites
¹/₄ teaspoon salt
1 cup sugar
³/₄ cup ground almonds
¹/₂ teaspoon almond extract

Cover the bottom of a cookie sheet with unglazed paper.

Beat egg whites and salt until frothy. Add sugar one spoonful at a time, beating thoroughly after each addition. Beat until stiff peaks are formed. Fold in the ground almonds with almond extract.

Drop by teaspoonfuls about one inch apart. Keep small and uniform. Bake at 350° for 20 minutes or until lightly browned.

RED AND WHITE PARTY
Valentine's Day

Goal: Church attenders will take part in activities that encourage interaction among a large number of people.

Main idea: Everyone will be asked to bring a dessert that is either red or white. The evening's activities are built around the red and white theme—food, games, Valentine thank-yous.

If your guests have difficulty thinking of red and white recipes, you might suggest a few, but much of the fun of this party will be deciding for themselves what would work.

RED AND WHITE RECIPES

ICE BOX CHERRY (or strawberry) PIE

8 ounces cream cheese
1 cup powdered sugar
1 package Dream Whip
1 teaspoon vanilla
1 can cherry pie filling
baked pie shell

Beat sugar and cream cheese. Prepare package of Dream Whip according to the directions and flavor with vanilla.

Fold the whip into the cheese mixture and pour into baked shell. Cover with 1 can of cherry pie filling. Add a few drops of red coloring, if you wish. Chill for 1 hour.

Or use frozen strawberries instead of cherries. Thaw and drain off juice. Add 3 Tablespoons sugar to juice; thicken with 2 Tablespoons cornstarch over low heat. Cool, add the strawberries, and pour on top.

CHERRY RICE PUDDING

5 1/2 quarts milk
3 cups rice
12 Tablespoons sugar
8 teaspoons vanilla
1/4 pound almonds
2 large cans dark pitted cherries, drained
1 1/2 quarts cream, whipped

Bring milk to boil. Stir in rice and cook under a lid for 45 minutes over very low flame. Take pot from stove and cool. Mix in sugar and vanilla when lukewarm. Stir occasionally. Grind almonds and add. Fold in drained cherries and whipped cream.

This serves 40. An idea: put just one whole almond in the pudding. Announce that the person who gets the whole almond must tell a story from his own life that is appropriate to Valentine's day.

RASPBERRY ICE CREAM PIE

1 1/3 cups crushed graham crackers
1/4 cup sugar
1/2 teaspoon cinnamon
1/8 teaspoon salt
1/3 cup butter, melted
1 quart vanilla ice cream
1 pint fresh or frozen raspberries

Mix crumbs with sugar, cinnamon, and salt. Blend in melted butter. Line a 9-inch pie pan with mixture, pressing firmly over bottom and sides of pan. Chill. Fill shell with a layer of ice cream. Top with raspberries, sweetened to taste. Add another layer of ice cream and top with berries. Serve at once, or keep in freezer until serving time. Serves about 6.

INVITATION IDEA
You may want to print the invitations on children's Valentines.

The colors of Valentine's Day
Come dressed in red and white
Bring a red or white dessert
Be prepared to tell what makes you turn
  red or white
When:
Where:

WHITE VALENTINE'S PIE
---

1 prepared pie shell
1 cup sugar
4 Tablespoons flour
1/2 teaspoon salt
1 1/2 cup milk
1 Tablespoon unflavored gelatin softened
   in 1/4 cup cold water
3/4 teaspoon vanilla
1/4 teaspoon almond extract
1/2 cup stiffly whipped cream
3 egg whites beaten
1/4 teaspoon cream of tartar
1/2 cup sugar
1 1/2 cups moist coconut

Mix 1 cup sugar, flour, salt in saucepan. Gradually stir in milk. Cook over low heat, stirring until it boils. Boil 1 minute. Remove from heat. Stir in softened gelatin. Cool. When partially set, beat with rotary beater until smooth. Blend in vanilla and almond extract.

Gently fold in whipped cream. Carefully fold in egg whites, cream of tartar, and 1/2 cup sugar. Then fold in 1 cup moist coconut.

Pile into cooled pie shell. Sprinkle with moist coconut and chill about two hours until set. Serve cold.

CHERRY NUT MUFFINS
---

2 cups sifted flour
1/2 teaspoon salt
3 teaspoons baking powder
1/2 cup sugar
1/2 cup water or cherry juice
1/2 cup chopped nuts
3 Tablespoons melted shortening
1/2 cup evaporated milk
1 beaten egg
1/3 cup chopped maraschino cherries
Optional for this party: add a few drops of
   red food coloring.

Sift dry ingredients together. Add nuts. Mix all liquids together. Add cherries. Blend into dry ingredients just until moistened. Bake in greased muffin pans at 350° for about a half hour. Makes 1 dozen muffins.

PIE CRUST
---

1 1/4 cup flour
1/4 teaspoon baking powder
1/2 teaspoon salt
1 stick shortening
3 or 4 Tablespoons cold milk or water

Cut flour into shortening that has been sifted with dry ingredients. Gradually add liquid until rolling consistency.
For a two-crust pie:
2 cups flour
1/2 teaspoon baking powder
3/4 teaspoon salt
1 cup shortening
4-6 Tablespoons milk or water
Follow instructions above.

CHERRY JELLO SALAD
---

2 small packages tapioca pudding
1 package small cherry Jello
2 3/4 cup water (minus two Tablespoons)
1 large container Cool Whip
1 large can drained cherries
1 small jar applesauce

Bring to boil the tapioca, Jello, and water. Let cool. Mix in Cool Whip. Add cherries and applesauce. Stir together. Chill for several hours.

PINK PATS

1 cup butter, softened
1 cup butter mints, crushed
2 cups all-purpose flour
food coloring (red—just for this party!)
1 Tablespoon sugar

In a large mixer bowl, cream butter at medium speed until light. Add crushed mints and flour. Add food coloring. Blend well at low speed. If necessary, chill dough for easier handling. On waxed paper, roll out or pat dough to a 9-inch square. Sprinkle with sugar. Cut into 1½-inch squares. Bake at 300° for 18-20 minutes. Do not overbake.

Chocolate variety (but not for this party!): Add 1 or 2 Tablespoons cocoa with flour.

PINK PARTY DESSERT

1 large package strawberry Jello
2 cups water
2 cups small marshmallows
1 small can crushed pineapple
1 cup chopped nuts
1 small container cottage cheese (½ pint)
1 large container Cool Whip

Heat Jello, water, and marshmallows until marshmallows are dissolved. Chill until Jello begins to set. Fold in pineapple, nuts, cottage cheese, Cool Whip. Refrigerate until set.

RED AND WHITE QUESTIONS

On your invitation you asked people to come prepared for red and white questions. In the first few minutes of the evening, ask everyone to find out from at least ten other people what things would be most likely to make them turn white and red. This is an interesting way to get people moving.

Nametags will also make the opening minutes of the party easier. Perhaps you could print names on inexpensive children's valentines.

RED AND WHITE TAFFY PULL

Divide the group into sets of two. One set makes red taffy and another white. I've been to several taffy pulls. Even when the taffy doesn't pull perfectly, the interaction has been fun.

This recipe for salt water taffy comes from Betty Crocker. One group will add red food coloring to the mixture.

1 cup sugar
½ cup light corn syrup
⅔ cup water
1 Tablespoon cornstarch
2 Tablespoons butter or margarine
1 teaspoon salt
2 teaspoons vanilla

Butter square pan, 8″ x 8″ x 2″. In 2-quart saucepan, combine sugar, corn syrup, water, cornstarch, butter, and salt. Cook over medium heat, stirring constantly, to 256° on candy thermometer (or until small amount of mixture dropped into very cold water forms a hard ball). Remove from heat; stir in vanilla (and food coloring). Pour into pan.

When just cool enough to handle, pull taffy until satiny, light in color, and stiff. If taffy becomes sticky, butter hands lightly. Pull into long strips, ½ inch wide. With scissors, cut strips into 1-inch pieces. Wrap pieces that aren't eaten immediately in waxed paper. (Candy must be wrapped to hold its shape). Makes about 1 pound.

RED LETTERS

Give each person a red pencil and white paper, and ask him to write a love or appreciation note to someone in the church who deserves a valentine from him. For example, a note could be written to the pastor or staff, Sunday school teacher, service planning people, college students who help in the nursery, missionaries, hospitalized people, and on and on goes the list.

Notes should be short. You might want to provide envelopes for sending those valentines that can't be delivered in person at the party.

ROSES ARE RED

Everyone will have an opportunity to direct ROSES ARE RED valentines to others at the party. Caution people as they develop these to be careful not to hurt anyone's feelings. These should be expressions of real appreciation or fun little ditties that say, "I like you."

Remember the original rhyme?

Roses are red.
Violets are blue
Sugar is sweet,
And so are you.

Here's one that might be directed at the pastor. It's fun and it wouldn't hurt his feelings.

Roses are red
Three words say a lot
You're known for preaching
But three words it's not!

Or how about this more genuine message to the Sunday school teacher of your children or grandchildren:

Roses are red.
Praises to the sky.
My children love you,
And so do I.

A READ RED STORY

Everyone gets a sheet of paper. The host reads some incomplete sentences and each person fills in the blank. Then he should fold his answer under and pass the sheet to the person on his right.

That person will fill in the next blank in the story without knowing what the first person has written. And so on until the end of the story.

The last person to get the sheet at the end of the story will open the whole sheet to see for the first time what everyone in the group has written. The host will then call on several people to fill in the blanks from their sheets as he rereads the incomplete story.

Here's the story. Lines such as different people may write have been included to give you an idea of how disjointed and fun the final story could be.

1. Red woke up one morning with the scarlet sun pouring through his window. He walked to his window, looked out, and turned white because there . . .
One possible answer: he saw his mother-in-law with eight suitcases. (Do not read the possible answers. This is just to give you an idea of what might happen at your party. Pause long enough after each question to allow people to write.)
2. He jumped up, and . . .

One possible answer: grabbed the aspirin bottle.

3. This called for some quick action so he . . .
One possible answer: had his car waxed.

4. Finally he calmed down. He said, "I think I'll . . ."
One possible answer: have a peanut butter sandwich.

5. Unfortunately, that wasn't such a good idea because . . .
   One possible answer: the golf course was flooded.

6. "What do you think is the matter with me, doctor?" he asked in exasperation. The doctor looked grave and said, " . . ."
   One possible answer: "I think you've got bunions."

7. Red was amazed, to say the least. He decided to get a second opinion, so he went to . . .
   One possible answer: the local pet store.

8. Unfortunately the original diagnosis was confirmed. He was told again that . . .
   One possible answer: He would have to take water pills.

9. His wife's opinion of the whole thing was . . .
   One possible answer: expressed in great gales of laughter.

10. Red always was one to bounce back, so after his eventful day, he went back to . . .
    One possible answer: polishing his shoes.

A LOOK AT MOTIVES

A look at our motives—or in other words, how to handle it when friends don't get as excited about a party as we do.

It happens. And when it does, we've found it can taint our enthusiasm for the whole event.

Jack and Kathy helped us. We invited them to a party they didn't think they would enjoy. Instead of coming up with a bogus engagement or begging off with splitting headaches, they came right out with the truth.

"We've had it with groups for a while. We just don't want to come. How about the four of us going out to dinner soon instead?"

Crunch! They were one of our favorite couples. We always enjoyed having them, and they seemed to fit in so perfectly. Now they had said bluntly that they didn't want to come. Jack and I seriously considered canceling the whole event.

Instead, we rethought what an invitation is. It's not an obligation. We wanted people to come—if they wanted to and if they would enjoy the evening. Actually, it was nice of Jack and Kathy to be honest with us and to reinforce their friendship by suggesting we double date soon.

People must have the freedom to say no just as we have the freedom to invite them.

How can we expect good things to happen among us and our guests if our attitude is, "Look at all these people having a wonderful time in our home. Isn't it great? Pat our backs"?

The important thing is to put God in control of our parties—not Marlene and Jack.

THANKSGIVING
Making One Big Family
Out of Little Ones

Goal: Singles, small families, foreign families without Thanksgiving traditions will combine resources at a Thanksgiving meal. Together everyone will praise God for his year of goodness.

Main idea: Everyone will provide one dish to add to the Thanksgiving meal; the host family will supply the turkey. By combining resources, the meal will not be expensive.

Jack and I decided to go through the church directory and invite all the singles, foreign families, and small families. We figured nearly everyone would have a place to go already, so we could safely invite as many as we wanted to.

We were flabbergasted when the calls from those who were coming began to arrive.

"Thanks so much," a woman from Australia said. "We'll all come. We were wondering how Americans did this holiday, but we never thought we'd have the chance to find out."

"We'll be there with the kids," another woman said. "We didn't have money for the trip to my folks' place in Georgia. It's great to have something special to do close to home."

A single guy announced that he'd bring real mashed potatoes. "I was feeling a little family-less," he said.

This Thanksgiving party is the only one we've had where I have no idea how many people actually showed up. It was in the neighborhood of sixty, give or take a dozen kids. When the crowd filled our place, Diana, the neighbor across the hall, opened her doors for the overflow. Then the lady upstairs opened her place. Thank goodness we lived in an apartment building! A house would never have been big enough.

NAMETAGS
A must! Ours were little drawings of fat pilgrims. Each said, "In case you've forgotten, I'm _____."

CHORAL READING
Before the meal, we gave all readers a copy of a Thanksgiving Choral reading. We had contacted a few friends before the meal, and they were ready with short testimonies.

Host: Lord, you have poured out amazing blessings on this land! You have poured down your blessings on the land and it yields its bountiful crops.

All: Lord, you have poured out amazing blessings on this land! Now bring us back to loving you.

Friend: Oh come, let us sing to the Lord! Give a joyous shout in honor of the Rock of our salvation!

All sing "Come Ye Thankful People Come."

Hostess: God said, "What I want from you is your true thanks."

Friend: Father, I thank you because . . . (This person should complete the sentence with a personal reason she has for thanking the Lord this year.)

All: Sing your praise accompanied by music from the harp. Let the cornets and trumpets shout! Make a joyful symphony before the Lord, our King!

183

INVITATION IDEA:

T   hanksgiving Invitation
H   ome—532 Hillside
A   t about 1:30 on Thanksgiving Day
N   ow don't forget to bring a covered dish
K   ids—don't leave home without them
S   ure hope you can come

RSVP

Let the sea in all its vastness roar
with praise! Let the earth and all those
living on it shout, "Glory to the Lord."
Friend: Glory to the Lord! Let the
waves clap their hands in glee, and the
hills sing out their songs of joy before
the Lord.
Friend: Father, I praise you because . . .
Friend: Glory to the Lord.
Friend: Father I praise you because . . .
All sing the doxology as the Thanksgiving
prayer.

And then we ate! There was more than
enough for all. Jack had made two
turkeys, and their total forty pounds was
perfect. Actually, with all the great
things others brought, I don't think
anyone would have minded if we had run
out of turkey. (Some of our neighbors
were retired couples who were spending
the holidays with their children. When
they heard about our enormous party,
four people offered their ovens even
though they wouldn't be able to attend.)

PILGRIM SCAVENGER HUNT

In between the main course and the
dessert, we needed to clear dozens of
people out of the apartments for a
few minutes so we would have space to
reorganize. So the entire group was
divided into Pilgrim Scavenger Hunt
groups. Children were all included. For
some adults, it was the first time
they had worked hand in hand with the
youngsters in our church. It was
fun to see these random people become
competitive, enthusiastic groups. They
all left cheering and insisting that
their group would be back first with all
the items needed to win the Pilgrim
Scavenger Hunt.

Here's the Scavenger hunt list we used.
It is adapted to the area in which we
lived—about two blocks from a railroad
track in a suburban community. Change
anything you couldn't find in your
community.

Pilgrim Scavenger Hunt
1. One wild turkey feather or
   unreasonable facsimile.
2. A Pilgrim's Pet Rock. Be prepared
   to demonstrate a trick it can do.
3. Ten different types of leaves
   from the dense forests hereabouts.
4. One forked stick that would be
   perfect for killing snakes.
5. One piece of post-Indian litter.
6. One hat camouflaged sufficiently
   to avoid detection in hostile Indian
   territory.
7. One coin of this kingdom.
8. One Thanksgiving carol sung
   before a neighbor's house. Have
   astonished neighbor sign his/her
   name here (not that Pilgrims are
   not to be trusted!).

   _____

9. One musket ball or one round
   button.
10. Any tree's berry.
11. Any small weed—roots and all—
    that grows down by the iron
    horse's tracks.
12. A four-line poem in rhyming
    couplet about Thanksgiving.

    _____
    _____
    _____
    _____

13. Number of steps around our
    settlement (this block). _____.

14. Piece of wood to add to winter's fuel supply.
15. A friendly hello to a Pilgrim stranger on the street. Name of the thrilled person: _____.
16. Names of all churches within five minutes of our front door.
17. Scalp count—one gray hair, one brown hair, one blond hair, one red hair.
18. Scout around—one thumb print in a mud ball.
19. Pilgrim panic—something growing outside that you could eat in a pinch.
20. Anything that rhymes with pie —and come back for dessert!

I had the first group back show what they had collected and then I awarded them each chocolate turkeys.

However, people from the losing groups were still complaining months later that they had written wonderful rhyming couplets and developed excellent rock tricks that they hadn't had an opportunity to show off. So if you copy our Thanksgiving party, don't copy our mistake. Wait until all groups are back, and then allow creative people from each group to share what they have done.

CREATIVE PUMPKIN
Halloween or Autumn Party

Goal: To provide an occasion at which people can have a good time getting to know each other better, and in the process demonstrate some of their creative abilities.

Basic idea: Guests are divided into pairs and given a pumpkin to carve. Prizes for the most creative finished pumpkins add an element of competition.

You'll need one pumpkin for every two guests. Look for the cheapest ones you can find. I got mine at a farm just a few miles outside the city. I bought eight rather large ones for a little more than a dollar each. I think the teenager who helped me load my car with them thought I had a terrible case of Halloween fever.

The night of the party, I had the pumpkins circling the table.

Each woman put her name in a bag, and after everyone had arrived, the men drew partners. The couples then rushed to the table to pick the perfect pumpkin that would win them the top prizes.

People had followed the invitation and brought amazing pumpkin decorations. One man, a woodcarver, had come with carved and painted wooden pieces to stick on his pumpkin's face. He created one of the most professional orange men I've ever seen.

I gave each pair a written set of directions.

1. *Carve your pumpkin.*
2. *Name the clever little thing and be ready to give a bit of its family background.*
3. *Teach it to do one trick and be ready to have it perform the trick for everyone here.*

186

INVITATION IDEA

Come carve with us.
We'll supply the pumpkins . . .
You bring extra materials that will make
    your pumpkin a winning wonder. (Corn
    cobs, bits of material, buttons, crepe
    paper, and . . .)
When:
Where:
Why: It's high time we laughed together!

The results were great fun. See if your guests can match what ours did.

One couple carved out the whole inside of the pumpkin and cut a female face on it. They stuck marshmallows over the head like little curls. The finishing touch was a candle inside. It was their trick that won them a prize. "This pumpkin," George explained, "is an oven. She invited you to pull off one of her curls, stick it in her mouth, and toast yourself a gooey, delicious marshmallow."

Another couple had made a lovely pumpkin face, but the main part of the creation was the arms and legs they made out of construction paper. To each appendage they attached string, and made a moving puppet. The pumpkin's trick was to kick at people who tried to steal him from the pumpkin patch.

Everyone was asked to vote for pumpkin winners. We used the following ballot:

Pumpkin with the best family tree: _____
Most talented pumpkin: _____
Most amazing pumpkin face: _____

Prizes? Come up with your own ideas, but try to keep the prizes as fun as the carving. For example:

Pumpkin with the best family tree—the makers will each get a bag of pumpkin seeds to grow more pumpkins of excellent quality.

Pumpkin with the most talent—a frozen pie crust for each originator because people who can create a talented pumpkin ought to be able to figure out a way to create an excellent pie as well.

Pumpkin with the most amazing face—a can of pumpkin pie filling to each carver. The filling might be used on the face each night as a face mask to keep the excellent face in good condition.

One of our guests was a librarian. She was so impressed with the creations that she wanted to put them on display in the children's section of the library. Funny thing—not all those adults would give up their pumpkins. It's amazing how attached a person can get to an orange face!

FOOD

Of course, you'll want to play up the pumpkin idea in the foods. How about one of these?

PUMPKIN PIE

1 9-inch pie shell, unbaked
1 1/2 cups canned pumpkin
1/2 cup brown sugar
1/2 cup granulated sugar
1 teaspoon cinnamon
1/4 teaspoon salt
1 Tablespoon flour
1/4 teaspoon cloves
1/4 teaspoon ginger
2 eggs, slightly beaten
1 cup milk

Mix. Pour into pie shell. Bake at 425° for 45 to 50 minutes.

PUMPKIN BREAD

4 eggs
1 cup vegetable oil
1 teaspoon nutmeg
1 teaspoon cinnamon
3 cups sugar
1 1/2 teaspoon salt
1 cup canned pumpkin
2/3 cup water
2 teaspoons soda
3 cups flour
3/4 cup white raisins

Beat first 6 ingredients together. Add the rest in order, one at a time. It will be easier if you beat the eggs first, then the oil and the spices, before adding the rest of the ingredients. Grease and flour three 1-pound tall coffee cans. Fill 2/3 full and bake 1 hour at 350°. Cool about 10 minutes in can before removing.

You'll have a delicious bread—almost like cake. Spread a little butter on the slices before serving.

PUMPKIN REFRIGERATOR DESSERT

2 cups graham cracker, vanilla wafer, or
   gingersnap crumbs
1/3 cup each: sugar, melted butter
1 pound marshmallows
1/3 cup milk
1 pound can pumpkin filling
1/3 cup sugar
3/4 teaspoon cinnamon
1/4 teaspoon each: ginger, salt
2 cups whipping cream, whipped

Combine crumbs, sugar, and butter; press in bottom of 13" x 9" x 2" pan. Melt marshmallows in milk in double boiler. Combine pumpkin, sugar, cinnamon, ginger, and salt. Blend in marshmallows; cool. Fold in whipped cream. Turn mixture into crumb crust. Chill until firm.

ICE CREAM PUMPKIN SQUARES

1 1/2 cups graham cracker or gingersnap
   crumbs
1/4 cup melted butter
1 cup canned pumpkin
1/2 cup brown sugar
1/2 teaspoon salt
1/2 teaspoon cinnamon
1/2 teaspoon ginger
1/4 teaspoon nutmeg
1 quart vanilla ice cream
Optional: whipped cream and chopped nuts

Mix crumbs and butter. Press into an 8" x 8" x 2" buttered pan. Save some crumbs for top. Combine sugar and spices with pumpkin; fold in soft ice cream. Pour into crumb crust. Freeze.

Cut into squares and top with crumbs, whipped cream, nuts.

PUMPKIN NUT BARS

1/2 cup shortening
1 cup brown sugar
2 eggs
1 teaspoon vanilla
1 cup sifted all-purpose flour
1 teaspoon cinnamon
1/2 teaspoon each: baking powder, soda
1/2 teaspoon each: ginger, nutmeg
2/3 cup canned pumpkin
1/2 cup chopped walnuts
Frosting:
1 1/2 cups confectioners' sugar
2 Tablespoons each: shortening, orange juice
1 Tablespoon grated orange rind

Cream shortening and sugar until light and fluffy. Add eggs and vanilla; beat thoroughly. Sift together dry ingredients; add to creamed mixture in thirds alternately with pumpkin, beating until smooth after each addition. Fold in nuts. Spread in a greased 13″ x 9″ x 2″ pan. Bake at 350° for 20 minutes. Cool.

To prepare frosting, combine ingredients; beat until smooth. Spread over baked dessert. Cut into bars.

PUMPKIN COOKIES

2 cups brown sugar
2 cups canned pumpkin
1 cup salad oil
2 teaspoons vanilla
4 cups sifted flour
2 teaspoons soda
2 teaspoons baking powder
1 teaspoon each: salt, cinnamon, nutmeg
1/2 teaspoon ginger
2 cups raisins
1 cup chopped nuts

In mixing bowl, beat together; sugar, pumpkin, oil, and vanilla. Sift dry ingredients together; add and stir until smooth. Blend in raisins and nuts. Drop by spoonfuls on oiled baking sheet. Bake at 350° for 12 to 15 minutes. Makes about 7 dozen soft, moist cookies. (No eggs needed.)

If baked in the summer, keep refrigerated.

SOME ADDITIONAL GAME IDEAS
Ghost Stories
If your pumpkin party is around Halloween time, ghost stories can be great fun. They allow guests to be ten and eleven years old again. Turn out all the lights and ask volunteers to tell stories they remember from their camping-trip-and-pajama-party days.

You might come prepared with one. How about "The Headless Horseman"?

Pass the Glop
This idea is a throwback to junior high days. Again, all the lights are turned out and the host couple passes Halloween goodies around the circle of guests for each to touch. Each person whispers to the next person what it is that is being passed.

There is absolutely no point to this activity, except it does bring back the creepy, crawly, giggling sensations that we're usually too adult to enjoy.

Think up your own horrors, but just to get you started: skinned grapes could be passed with the whispered explanation, "eyeballs." Or a piece of liver could be passed as . . .be creative. The more adolescent, the better!

CREATIVE SNOWMEN
An Alternative
to the Creative Pumpkin
A "Creative Snowmen" party can break the winter blahs. It follows the same idea as the "Creative Pumpkin" party, but in this party people will be asked to decorate snowmen. Use the same goal as the "Creative Pumpkin." But this time you provide Styrofoam balls which will become the base of snow people. Each person should bring scraps, pins, buttons, whatever to help decorate his snowman.

Divide people in the same way you did the "Creative Pumpkin" party, and make the appropriate changes in your directions. For example:

1. Build and decorate your snowman.
2. Name the clever little thing and be ready to give a bit of his family background.
3. Teach it to do one trick.

Prize suggestions for the following categories:

1. Best name and background—prize would be a snow scene in a cheap frame.
2. Talented snowman—an ice cream scooper for making lots of clever snow or ice cream designs.
3. Most amazing facial features—a gift certificate from an ice cream store.

SOME ADDITIONAL GAME IDEAS FOR A SNOW PARTY
Can You Top This?

Everyone in snow country has a snow story. Start with one of your own, and encourage people to try to top it.

Give a prize to the person who has the top-of-the-topped story.

This year, Jack and I might win! He was in the middle of Chicago when last year's big storm hit. He got stuck getting out of his parking place. So he jumped out to push the car, slammed and locked the door, leaving the motor running. He ended up breaking a window to get back inside. By the time he had gotten home more than fifteen inches of snow had fallen, and he claimed he was almost frozen. Can you top that?

Snow Charades

Divide the group into teams. A person from each team takes turns pulling a snow related word or phrase from a bag and trying to communicate the word or phrase to his teammates by drawing it. He is not allowed to speak or give any signs. He just keeps drawing until someone guesses or until his time —60 seconds—runs out.

Keep track of seconds, and the team with the fewest seconds wins.

Some snow ideas that you might place in the bag for this game are:

tundra
reindeer
"Walking in a Winter Wonderland"
igloo
"I'll Be Home for Christmas"
snow removal crews

FOOD
Ice cream makes sense. How about ice cream sundaes? Or if you're having this party with a lot of teenagers, you might want to have crushed ice snow cones.

PEPPERMINT ICE CREAM

3/4 cup honey
1/2 teaspoon sea salt
2 cups milk
1 Tablespoon mint extract
4 cups thick cream

Put all but the cream in a pan. Heat just until small bubbles appear around the edges. Cool to lukewarm. Freeze several hours until mushy. Beat smooth. Whip cream until wavy. Blend in the milk and honey mixture until well blended. Freeze until firm, stirring often the first few hours.

191

8

LET THERE BE SHOWERS

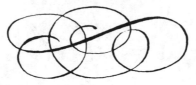

INVITATION SUGGESTION

We're honoring _____ and _____
   at a Bride and Groom Shower.
When:
Where:
Send us a slide or photograph of your own
   wedding, and come prepared to share
   one interesting thing that happened that
   day. Singles, send a picture of yourself and
   come prepared with advice to give the
   couple—something you've learned by
   observing married friends!

I WAS TWENTY-THREE years old before it dawned on me that a shower didn't have to be an all-woman activity. All-women showers can be great fun—my own wedding shower was one. But men can have as much fun at a shower as women.

Think about it. Most showers are an affirmation of a couple or family—a wedding shower or a baby shower. In both cases, the woman is only half of the big doings. Why not include the man in the party, and his friends, as well?

When I was in grad school, I attended a church where the college group was almost entirely made up of students living away from home. So when one of the men in the group set the date with a girl back home, the group discussed the possibility of throwing a shower just for him. We giggled a lot. Somehow it didn't feel right to be honoring the man. But our better sense took over, and we had a great party honoring him and his life-changing decision. He got some excellent gifts—a man's apron, a screwdriver kit, some house plant tools, and a subscription to *Apartment Living*.

So I'm suggesting that for all these showers, you consider coed participation.

FOR THE BRIDE AND GROOM SLIDE INTO MARRIAGE

Goal: To honor the engaged couple and affirm the church's support of their decision to live for Christ together.

THE GIFT
At a large shower, the process of opening fifteen to twenty gifts can be tedious.

I've found that when everyone contributes to one gift, the interaction time at the shower can be longer, more fun. It also allows the group to make a substantial contribution to the couple, providing them with something they really want. Kris and Tom, for example, asked that we get them zip-together sleeping bags, an expensive gift that was possible when we divided the cost twenty ways.

SLIDE INTO MARRIAGE PREPARATION

Part One—Slides of the Couple
The host should try to get representative pictures of the life of the couple, hopefully without them knowing it. Gladys did this for my shower. She got my mother to donate pictures of me diapered, learning to walk, on my first date—wrong guy, graduating from high school, early pictures of Jack and me. As she showed the slides she shared bits of our history so that the people attending learned a little more about Jack and me and could participate more fully in the big step we were about to take.

Most of the pictures my mother provided were photographs that Gladys had made into slides, a more effective way of sharing the pictures with the whole group than passing around snapshots.

Part Two—Slides of Guests
The host couple should get these pictures made into slides and placed into some order in preparation for showing them and having guests share advice the night of the shower.

SUGGESTED ORDER
FOR THE PARTY

Slides of the Couple

Work up a little talk about the slides of
the couple. For example, "Here's a
picture of baby Jack at the seashore with
his bucket and shovel. Off to the right,
are the local bathing beauties. You can
see how unimpressed he is. My, how times
have changed!" Keep this part of the
evening light, fun.

PRESENTATION OF THE
GIFT OR GIFTS

Guest slides

As the slides of guests' weddings flash
on the screen, people should share one
funny thing that happened in preparation for or on the day of their weddings.
Almost everyone had something unusual
happen. For example, "My flower girl
threw all her petals by the time she got to
the middle of the church. Then she
turned around and started picking them
up again, so she would have more to
throw at the front half of the church."
Or, "In the receiving line, I was
introducing one of my relatives to my
mother-in-law and my mind went blank. I
could not remember her name."

Singles should share one of the things
they have learned about marriage by
observing married couples around them.
Show their pictures on the screen
as they talk. Again, encourage them to
keep it light.

Panel on Marriage

Place four chairs at the front of the room.
Draw the names of four guests out of a
hat. Introduce them as great experts on
marriage, and explain that you will be
interviewing them on the subject of
their expertise. Make sure everyone
knows this is not a serious activity. The
funnier the panel is, the better.

After a panel has answered two or
three questions, retire them and pick
another group of four.

Use questions like these:

1. One of the biggest decisions young
   married people have to make is
   who will take out the garbage.
   Could you give us some weighty
   words on how to solve this
   dilemma?
2. I understand that most men like
   eggs over easy in the morning.
   Could you give some directions to
   the bride on the best way to make
   them?
3. If you surveyed 1,000 people
   who have been married for twenty-
   five years or more, what do you
   think would be the three most
   common reasons they would give
   for their success?
4. Experts say it's important for a
   couple to continue to date each
   other after they are married.
   What's your opinion of this?
5. Wedding services can be hard on
   the groom. What advice do you
   have for him?
6. I've heard it said that there are
   three or four things a woman just
   won't stand for. The groom ought
   to know what they are so he won't
   get off to a bad start. Can you clue
   him in?
7. Usually one half of the couple is
   neater than the other half. What
   do you suggest to the disorderly

part of this marriage team?

8. Finish this sentence: You will never have trouble with your in-laws if you . . .

9. Usually the bride and groom get a lot of suggestions on places they might go for a honeymoon. Where would you suggest and why?

10. Sometimes if people know what might cause fights they can avoid them. Can you tell us the three things married couples argue most about.

Pair on Marriage

Switch the process around now, and put the bride and groom-to-be in the chairs in front of the group and allow the guests to ask the engaged couple questions. Let the couple know they have veto power; they don't have to answer all questions.

I've done this at several showers and have never had anyone ask a question that was in poor taste. Instead people ask questions like, "Where did you meet?" "What did you think of Rita the first time you met her?" "How did you feel the first time you met your mother-in-law?" "Who proposed?"

A Prayer Pact

A shower is a fun occasion for Christians to say, "Yes, we affirm your decision to marry." A prayer pact can be an important part of that affirmation. The host will want to have copies of this pact for people present, and they should read it together to the couple and to God.

Here's a sample. Edit it to most perfectly fit your situation.

PRAYER PACT

All to the couple: We, your Christian church family, are pleased that you are getting married. We have watched your relationship grow and smiled with you through your happy days of getting to know each other better.

Marriage is a difficult and totally rewarding vocation. In no other way can two people better share their lives and expand their ministries together. We know, some of us from experience, how difficult the days ahead may be. It will be helpful on those days for you to remember that you are not in this marriage alone. You are loved and cared for by us—your friends, your church family.

In return, you have a responsibility to us, to share with us when you have needs or when you want to be uplifted in special prayer. You are accountable to God and to us to make your marriage work—to make it an example of Christ at work in our community.

Host: Father, we bring _____ and _____ before you. Tonight we celebrate their coming marriage. Give them a special love for each other that will continue to grow through the years. Thank you, Lord, for your wonderful plan of marriage. Thank you for all the gifts that are part of marriage, and for the responsibilities that are part of it as well. Shower your blessings on _____ and _____ as surely as we have showered them tonight with our gifts and celebration. Amen.

Refreshments
Anything from a full covered-dish
supper to simple dessert will work
perfectly. It might also be the time to do
some novelty things with food. Here
are some ideas we have collected through
the years. They take time to do, but
they are fun and seem to fit with the
festive mood of wedding showers.

Pimento Carrot
Pimento cheese rolled into a shape of a
carrot—add a sprig of parsley as the
stem.

Egg Shell Basket
Hollow egg shells out into the shape of
baskets. Fill with candy. Tie with ribbon.

Candle Holder
Tie a ribbon around a marshmallow.
Attach a Lifesaver as a handle. Stick a
tiny candle in the marshmallow.

Celery Curls
Cut celery ribs into 3-inch lengths,
making parallel slits at one end. Have the
slits narrow and reaching almost to
the other end of the piece of celery. Cover
with icy-cold water and refrigerate
until the cut ends curl.

Stuffed Radishes
Hollow out some good-sized radishes and
fill with sweet butter or cheese spread.

Carrot Curls
Use large, crisp carrots. Peel and cut off
lengthwise slices to make flat surfaces.
Cut off thin strips with vegetable peeler.
Soak in ice water and they will curl.

Fruit Baskets
Select large oranges or grapefruits with
thick skin. Cut fruit in half, and remove
segments. Remove pulp from the shells.
Mix grapefruit or oranges with other
fruits and refill the shells. Chill in the
refrigerator. Just before serving, sprinkle
each basket with ginger ale. Top with
whipped cream.

TANGRAM SHOWER
Goal: To honor the engaged couple and
affirm the church's support of their
decision to live for Christ together.

At our Tangram Shower for Kris and
Tom, we were flabbergasted at the
variety of interesting shapes and advice
they got. We put the sheets into a
scrapbook for them. (See illustration.)

Remember, you will have to cut
tangram pieces for each invitation;
include one sample of a finished tangram
just to get people thinking. (See my
sample.)
If people tape the pieces on a piece of
construction paper, make your tangrams
from squares no bigger than 4" x 4".

SUGGESTED ORDER
FOR THE PARTY
Tangram Advice
Everyone should go around the room
and share his tangram and advice with
the couple. Encourage everyone to
write his advice on the tangram and sign
his name so the couple will have these
fun and serious advice pictures as a
treasure of the evening.

INVITATION IDEA

Tangram Shower

Tangram:
Shower for:
When:
Where:

A square that has been cut into these 7 pieces.

In this invitation, you'll find a cut tangram.
Please arrange the pieces on a piece of
construction paper to illustrate some advice
you would like to give the engaged couple.

Write your advice on your tangram.

Illustration:

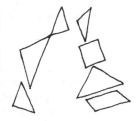

*Never go
to sleep
without
a goodnight
kiss*

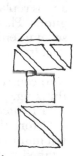

*Marriage is
a growing,
shining
trophy
as long as
it points
to Christ.*

Make sure everyone tells what his tangram means. Most tangrams are symbolic and won't make a lot of sense until the developer shares what he meant by the arrangement of the seven pieces.

I've Got a Marriage Secret
After you know who will be coming to the shower, ask several to come up with marriage secrets, preferably ones they haven't shared with anyone.

The host should act as moderator for this activity patterned after the television game show, "I've Got a Secret."

Three members from the party should be panelists. Panelists take turns asking questions that can be answered with a yes or no until the secret is guessed. When it is, that panelist is awarded a prize and is replaced by someone else from the guests. Play as many guests as people seem to enjoy.

Here are some ideas for secrets. You might want to share them with the people who contribute secrets, just to get them thinking.

"I fainted at my wedding reception."

"I tore the hem of my wedding gown ten minutes before I went up the aisle, so I taped it up for the ceremony."

"I was engaged four times before I finally got married."

FOOD
Why not serve sheet cakes that have been cut into tangram shapes? People would cover their tangram shape with a variety of toppings—whipped cream, fruit, chocolate sauce, etc.

STANDARD SHEET CAKE
---
1 cup shortening
2 cups sugar
4 eggs, separated
3 cups flour
3 teaspoons baking powder
1 cup milk
1¹/2 teaspoon vanilla
Cream shortening and sugar, mixing thoroughly. Add beaten egg yolks. Sift flour and measure. Sift with baking powder. Add alternately with milk. Add vanilla and fold in stiffly beaten egg whites. Bake at 375° for 35 to 40 minutes.

MINI IDEAS
You can build complete parties around the following ideas, or simply add them to whatever other shower ideas you have.

Around-the-Clock Gifts
Each person is assigned a time on a twenty-four-hour clock—all time slots don't have to be filled. He is responsible for selecting a gift for the couple that could be used at his time of day. So if he is assigned (or picks) 7 A.M., he might bring an egg coddler. Gifts are opened in sequence, starting at 1 A.M.

Fatten the Couple
Each guest brings a favorite dish and a copy of the recipe for that dish. The recipes are collected and put into a newly-wed book.

This is an excellent idea for a group in which buying a gift would cause difficulty or when gifts are not necessary or appropriate.

Calendar Party
Each guest signs a year's calendar, picking an evening when he would like to do something with the newly married couple as his guests. Especially if the couple is well acquainted with everyone, this is a good idea.

Money Tree
Often nothing is more needed or appreciated than money. Ask each person to bring a gift of money in single dollar bills. Fold each dollar in accordion style and tie it tightly around the middle with thread. Then fan the edges to look like leaves. Tie the money to a tree branch and present it to the couple at the party.

MA AND PA INITIATION
A Shower for the First Baby
Goal: Christian friends will celebrate the coming baby event, and pray together for the new family.

BABY GIFTS
Be creative here. There are a lot of gifts that take little money and add tremendously to the lives of the new parents. I know one completely broke medical student who threw a shower for his best friends. He gave them a handful of "Free Baby-sitting Tickets." Not only was his gift worth a financial fortune at today's baby-sitting prices, it represented a creative approach to gift-giving.

You might want to consider giving one large shower gift rather than individual small ones. The single gift takes only minutes to open and allows more time for interaction with the couple and others at the party than does the time-consuming opening of single gifts.

Sometimes buying one large gift can be a problem. Again be creative. I had one friend who was so excited about the baby that by shower time, she and her husband had bought everything the new child could need. So the shower guests all contributed money to a baby bank account and presented the savings book to the parents at the party.

Here's my suggested order for a Ma and Pa Initiation shower. Cut and add things that would make the party perfect for your group and your honored couple.

INITIATION MIMES
Mime comes from the Greek word "to imitate." In a mime, a person acts out an action or experience without using words. Mime allows us to use our facial and body expressions to communicate the meaning of the occasion.

The host couple should announce that a number of authorities on baby care are going to mime different activities that would be helpful for expectant parents to know about.

(You may want to assign these mimes before the party so people have time to practice once in front of a mirror. No props unless absolutely necessary.)

Here are some mime activities you might assign: You announce the topic, and the actor proceeds to demonstrate the activity. Encourage participants to be as funny as possible.

1. _____ will now demonstrate how to change a diaper—a very dirty diaper. (The more hammed

INVITATION IDEA

Shower for _____ and _____,
   the soon-to-be parents
When:
Where:
We'll be dedicating this evening to parent
   training—giving the new parents a
   running start on the next eighteen years!

up the better! After all, anything for a little ma-and-pa education.)

2. _____ will demonstrate how to get strained spinach down an unwilling baby's throat.

3. _____ and _____ will show the new parents the proper routine to follow when baby starts crying in the middle of the night.

(For this, the couple may want to set two chairs in front of the group. The chairs represent beds. The humor will come as each person does his or her best to make the other get out of the bed to take care of the baby's needs.)

4. _____ will demonstrate how to dress the baby to go out into the cold winter.

5. _____ will show you how a parent looks as he or she is trying to coax baby into his first step.

6. _____ and_____ will demonstrate what happens the first time you take baby to a restaurant.

(You might want to use chairs. Set them facing each other as if there were a table between them. The miming couple should pretend their baby is in a high chair. Other imaginary people would include the waitress and customers.)

7. Your baby will have to learn to enjoy many different people. Let's suppose the proud parents have taken him for a walk through the park. _____ will play three different people who come by to look into the buggy. First, a sweet, little grandmother. Next, a tough teenage boy. Finally, a mother with a baby about the same age.

8. _____ will demonstrate how you'll feel at night when you look at the little darling fast asleep in his crib.

(Use this as the final mime. The actor should simply stand, sigh in pure joy, and sit down again.)

GIVE THE PARENTS-TO-BE THE GIFTS

Plan a little initiation ceremony for the parents. Ask them to come up to the front of the room. Explain that this initiation will help them get ready for the great things to come—a preview of what babying is all about.

You'll be handing the parents various things throughout this initiation. Explain each one as you add it to the load the parents are holding. When you have completed the initiation, you should take a picture of the couple. It will look great in a baby book.

1. Hand the father something that weighs twenty pounds. Explain that before long, he'll be able to carry this weight for miles without thinking twice.

2. Present the mother with a well-spotted apron. Point to each spot and explain what it is. For example, "This is plum pudding. The baby burped at the wrong time. And this is red nail polish. You were trying to rock the baby with one hand and put polish on the other two hands and the fourth hand got flustered when you rubbed the apron! And this yellow spot with the strange smell—well, that's something else!" Really get into

this. Finally ask the mother-to-be to put the apron on. (Make sure it's big enough.)

3. Bring someone up from the watching guests, and ask that person to pull the mother's hair just a little but rather continuously. Babies have a way of doing this, and it's good to be prepared.
4. Give the father a large damp towel. Explain that drippy babies are the norm, and a wise father gets used to the slightly damp, uncomfortable feeling.
5. Present the father with a number of pins and ask him to hold them in his mouth. Explain that this is how many people keep track of the pins while they are changing the damp youngster. After a few months, assure him, the father will find his lips toughened to pin pricks.
6. Give the mother a book about child rearing. Have her hold it open. Explain that this is a book on practically anything she wants to know about her baby. It's as comforting as it is important to know what the book says each step of the way. (You might want to pick a good book, and add this to the parents' presents for the evening.)
7. Give the mother a pacifier to hold in her mouth. Explain that this is usually for the baby, but there may be days when she wishes she had one too.
8. Give the father a bottle, and ask him to test it on his wife's wrist to determine whether the temperature is right for baby. If she turns red on that spot, it's too hot. If she

turns blue, it's too cold. If she can hardly tell that she's being sprinkled, it's absolutely perfect.
9. Give the parents a banner on a stick that reads, "Now Ready for Parenthood!"

PRAYER FOR
THE PARENTS-TO-BE
Ask several fathers and mothers to pray over the couple. Encourage them to be personal in their prayers—praying specifically for areas of problems and joys in the years to come. Here are two examples. Read them to the parents who will be praying to give them an idea of how personal you want them to be.

"Father, I remember how wonderful I felt when I discovered that I would be a father. I was scared to death. Babies are so little and seem so breakable. Be with (father) as he gets used to his new name and role. May he perform it with love and consideration. May he know that the gift of fatherhood comes from you, and it is among the most precious gifts you give."

"Dear Heavenly Father. When our baby was born, I didn't care if she was a boy or a girl or if her eyes were blue or her hair curly. All I wanted was for her to be whole. You answered my prayer. I pray your health upon the baby that _____ and _____ will have. May the child be perfect, mentally and physically. Thank you for your amazing gift of tiny life."

REFRESHMENTS
The mother-to-be would probably appreciate something light that won't

show up on her next weigh-in at her doctor's visit. So how about:

COTTAGE CHEESE LIGHT DESSERT

1/2 package lime low-calorie gelatin
1 1/2 Tablespoons liquid calorie-free
   sweetener
1/4 teaspoon salt
3 eggs, separated
1 1/2 cups skim milk
3 cups cottage cheese
1 Tablespoon lemon juice
1 teaspoon vanilla
1 can crushed pineapple, drained

Place gelatin, sweetener, and salt in top of a double boiler. Beat egg yolks with milk until blended. Mix with gelatin; cook, stirring constantly, until mixture is slightly thickened. Chill until partly set. Beat cheese in electric blender or with electric mixer until smooth. Stir in lemon juice and vanilla. Fold in gelatin mixture and pineapple. Beat egg whites until stiff but not dry. Fold into gelatin. Turn into a 9" x 9" x 2" pan. Chill until firm.

A few more calories, but maybe the mother-to-be will splurge:

STUFFED PEACHES

6 large, firm peaches
1/2 cup macaroon crumbs
1/2 cup almonds
4 Tablespoons sugar
1 Tablespoon candied orange peel
1/3 cup peach juice

Halve the peaches. Combine macaroon crumbs, chopped almonds, 2 Tablespoons sugar, and candied peel. Lightly fill the peach halves. Place in baking dish. Pour peach juice over peaches.

Sprinkle on remaining sugar. Bake at 350° for 15 minutes. Serve hot or cold.

AUNT LILLIAN'S FRUIT SALAD

1 or 2 large cans of fruit cocktail
1 can crushed pineapple
1 jar maraschino cherries
1 1/2 cups tokay grapes
2 cups miniature marshmallows
6 bananas
4 ounces pecan meats
2 4-ounce cartons whipping cream
6 ounces cream cheese

Open cocktail, pineapple, and cherries. Drain well. Cut cherries in quarters. Halve grapes and pit them. Add, with marshmallows, bananas, and chopped-up pecans, to other fruit.

Whip cream—not too stiff—just until it is wavy. Cut up softened cream cheese and add in chunks as you whip the cream. Pour over fruit. If dressing is too thick, add just enough milk to reach the desired consistency.

And just in case you want to break the calorie bank, here are a few desserts your skinny guests will love:

FUDGE BROWNIES

2 ounces unsweetened chocolate
1/3 cup corn oil
1 cup sugar
2 eggs
3/4 cup sifted flour
1/2 teaspoon baking powder
1/2 teaspoon salt
1/2 cup broken pecans

Melt chocolate with oil over hot water. Beat in sugar and eggs. Sift dry ingredients and stir in. Mix in nuts. Spread in greased pan and bake 30 to 35 minutes at 350°. Do not overbake. When the brownie mixture is slightly cool, cut into 16 2-inch squares.

THREE-LAYER FUDGE CAKE

2 1/4 cups sifted cake flour
1 teaspoon baking soda
1/2 teaspoon salt
4 ounces chocolate
1 1/4 cup milk
3/4 cup brown sugar
1 teaspoon vanilla
2/3 cup shortening
1 cup granulated sugar
3 eggs

Sift flour, soda, and salt together. Heat chocolate and milk in top of double boiler until chocolate melts. Add brown sugar and beat until smooth. Cool and add vanilla. Cream shortening with granulated sugar until fluffy. Add eggs one at a time, beating thoroughly after each. Add sifted dry ingredients and chocolate mixture alternately in small amounts, beating well after each addition. Bake at 350° in 3 round cake pans for about 1/2 hour.

Top with your favorite frosting.

PEANUT BUTTER BANANA PIE

1 3 1/4-ounce package vanilla pudding and
* pie mix*
1 1/2 cups miniature marshmallows
1/2 cup heavy cream, whipped
2 bananas, sliced
lemon juice
peanut butter crust

Prepare pie filling as directed on package, except using 1 3/4 cups milk. Cover with waxed paper; chill.

Fold in marshmallows and whipped cream. Dip bananas in lemon juice, place in crust. Pour filling over bananas. Chill several hours. Garnish with additional banana slices, whipped cream, and peanuts, if desired.

PEANUT BUTTER CRUST

3 cups miniature marshmallows
1/2 cup crunchy peanut butter
1/4 cup margarine
4 cups corn flakes

Melt marshmallows with peanut butter and margarine in saucepan over low heat. Stir until melted and well blended. Remove from heat. Stir in cereal until well coated. Press onto bottom and sides of a greased 9-inch pie plate, and chill.

MINI IDEAS

You can build complete parties around the following ideas, or simply add them to whatever other shower ideas you have.

NEW GROWTH
ON THE FAMILY TREE
Do a little family research by contacting the parents and grandparents of the couple. Write a short history for the baby, and actually read it to "him" at the party. You might start like this. "Baby, you are being born into a wonderful family. Did you know that your great-grandfather on your mother's side was considered the best woodworker in Gap? And on your father's side, your great grandfather was a farmer who loved God

so much that he was willing to give up his farm and move to a new country when his government tried to limit the amount of time he could spend in church . . ."

You might add a touch of "This Is Your Life" by having a few surprise guests appear as you read the baby's history. For example, the soon-to-be grandparents could remain in another room until it was time for them to "appear" and tell their part in the baby's history.

BABY GUESS

Baby Guess is a perfect way to add a little excitement to the coming event when there isn't time or money for a shower. Or, perhaps it's not the first baby, but you would still like to do something a little special for the parents. (Our church had a rule that the church sponsored only first baby showers. Before the rule, we were feeling the crunch of buying

several gifts a month.)

For a baby guess, find out when the baby is due and make up time sheets for the few days before and after that date. Ask people if they would like to guess when the baby will come at $1.00 a guess.

We did this for Larry and Juanita and their third baby. I was amazed at how seriously people took this game. Almost everyone asked questions before they would sign. "What was her pattern with the other two children?" "What did the doctor say on her last checkup?"

We collected about $40, and the complete amount went to the couple to help with baby bills. We also had a little prize for the person who guessed closest to the baby's actual birth hour. That prize was won by a fellow who is about to become a father himself for the first time.

We set up our sheets like this:

WEDNESDAY

1 A.M. _____
3 A.M. _____
Larry Brook
7 A.M. _____
10 A.M. _____
2 P.M. *Brian Dill*
Gabby Garcia
5 P.M. _____
10 P.M. _____

And then on to the next day.

This little technique required very little time, and practically no money. But it generated a lot of enthusiasm and support for the parents. Everyone had a small, personal stake in the arrival of the new baby.

AROUND THE CLOCK BABY GIFTS
(Also suggested for an engagement party) Each person is assigned a time on a twenty-four-hour clock (all times don't have to be filled). He is supposed to buy a gift that could be used by the baby or baby's parents at that time of the day or night. For example, if he were assigned 4 A.M., he might give the parents a bottle warmer. And, of course, diapers would fit any slot.

PICTURE GUESS
Everyone should bring one of his own baby pictures. The host couple should put the pictures on a table and number each. Everyone gets pencil, paper, and the job of guessing which picture goes with which adult.

BABY SHOWER GAMES
There are a lot of silly games that can make a party more lively. Here are three suggestions.

Diaper relay: You'll need two life-sized dolls and two diapers. Both teams line up, and at the whistle the first person in each team rushes up to the baby and completely diapers it—two pins and all. He runs back and tags the next person in line. That person comes up to the doll and undiapers it. He goes back and tags the next person who diapers it, and so on until one line is finished.

You can add all sorts of extras—like a little mustard on the diaper!

Baby Feeding Exhibition: Blindfold the father-to-be and get a volunteer from the guests who is also to be blindfolded. (You might pick the last person to become a father.) Then have them feed each other. Pick some baby food that's a terrible color. The results are funny—if you like messy fathers.

Baby Food Testing: Divide the group into pairs. Blindfold one person in each pair. The other will give the blindfolded person one taste of a baby food, and the other must identify it. He should whisper his answer to his partner, who will keep track of correct answers. The person with the most correct answers wins—how about a jar of slightly used baby food?

You won't have to have more than one jar of each flavor because people don't have to be tasting the same food at the same time. Just pass the jars.